## OPTIMAL BUSINESS SERIES

# 1001 BUSINESS IDEAS

## Finding the Right Business to Fuel Your Passion and Create Your Perfect Lifestyle

## Bob Armstrong

Copyright © 2018

# 1001 BUSINESS IDEAS

## FINDING THE RIGHT BUSINESS TO FUEL YOUR PASSION AND CREATE YOUR PERFECT LIFESTYLE

## BOB ARMSTRONG

# 1001 BUSINESS IDEAS

Finding the Right Business to Fuel Your Passion and Create Your Perfect Lifestyle

## Bob Armstrong



Independently Published

First Edition

ISBN: 9781980901570

Ultimate Business Series

Modesto, California

# Disclaimer

All attempts have been made to verify the information in this book; however, neither the author, nor the publisher assumes any responsibility for errors, omissions, or contrary interpretations of the content within.

This book is for entertainment purposes only, and so the views and opinions of the author should not be taken as expert instruction or commands. The reader is responsible for his or her actions.

To obtain advice on financial or legal situations, please contact a qualified accountant or attorney. This book is not intended to offer professional advice. Rather it's to provide ideas for business start-up.

Neither the author nor the publisher assumes any responsibility or liability on behalf of the purchaser or reader of this book.

# Buyer Bonus Material

As of a way of thanking you for your purchase I've included a bonus report at the **end of this book**. I hope you enjoy this. Thank you.

# Other Books to Check Out

As part of the **Optimal Health Series** please pickup your copy of these books from Bob Armstrong too. Thank you!

Other Books Slated To Come Out Soon:

**1001 Business Ideas-** Finding the Right Business to Fuel Your Passion and Create Your Perfect Lifestyle

**Quit Smoking Now**

**Personal Food, Diet & Fitness Journal**

# Contents

# Dedication

I dedicate this book to YOU. You are probably a diligent, hard-working, dreamer who wants to make a difference with your life while making a contribution to others, and would like to be financially free as the result. May you find an idea in the pages of this book that will motivate you to action and create that special something that gets you up excited every day? That is my sincerest hope for you. Thank you and good luck in your quest dear friend.

Also, this is dedicated to my family and friends, who have supported me, witnessed (and even lived through) my entrepreneurial endeavors and ventures over the years. Special love and thanks to my amazing, patient and eternal companion Denise, who is my rock. Without her, none of this matters. Also to each of my children (Bob, Amy, Travis and Marybeth) who are so entrepreneurial and talented in their own ways. I so admire their courage to step out and begin new ventures and succeed so easily. They each inspire me and love them for it.

Bob

# Preface

I have been a "serial entrepreneur" all of my life. For as long as I can remember, I've had a business minded spirit. I was always looking for ways to make extra money, even as a kid growing up in Hayward. When I was 8 years old, I'd run carnivals and fairs in the backyard of my Hayward home and invite all of my neighborhood friends to come and spend some money. Everyone always had a good time and I always made enough money for my summer time activities.

I delivered newspapers while going to college and working a fulltime job in a restaurant as a manager. Those 600 newspapers almost killed me over a five year stint, but I loved it and I needed the money when I got married and four children came along.

Running a small business in today's world is almost a necessity to stay a step ahead, to be able to write off taxes and create a second or third income. But today's world has changed dramatically from the early 60's and 70's when I was young man. Just the thought of running an online business today for most folks is just standard protocol. No big deal. Twenty five years ago almost unheard of. I've always like the expression, "what do you know today that you didn't know 20 years ago?" "The answer is...everything!"

With the creation of the world-wide-web in 1989 and its development in the early to mid-1990's, I felt a shift then in the possibilities that the Internet could provide. I was one of the first in my community to get into computers and to sell information products from and CompuServe. It was thrilling. An easier mail-order so to speak, and with so many possibilities.

The business world is rapidly changing, and for us to benefit from the changes, we must learn to see the world differently and adapt. So, we have to think differently from what we believed even just a few short years ago in order to adapt and thrive.

Today we see entire industries being replaced by the technology wave that is here. Look at newspapers, the film and music industry today for example? See how consumers are now getting their news, their entertainment and music. Here's a list of 20 industries that have been changed dramatically because of the technology advances. The list below is from Adam Hays, CFA and was reported on **https://www.investopedia.com**. Check out the industry displace-ment.

- Travel websites such as **Expedia, Kayak,** and **Travelocity** have eliminated the need for **human travel agents. Check out WorldVentues**. This has become the largest travel club in the world. WV has taken travel to a new world class level.

- **Tax software such as TurboTax and Tax Act** have eliminated tens of thousands of jobs for **tax accountants.**

- **Newspapers** have seen their circulation numbers decline steadily, replaced by online media and blogs. Increasingly, computer software is actually writing news stories, especially local news and sporting event results.

- **Language translation** is becoming more and more accurate, reducing the need for human translators. The same goes for dictation and proof-reading.

- **Secretaries, phone operators, and executive assistants** are being replaced by enterprise software, automated telephone systems, and mobile apps.

- Online bookstores such as **Amazon** have forced **brick and mortar booksellers** to close their doors permanently. Additionally, the ability to self-publish and to distribute e-books is negatively affecting publishers and printers.

- **Financial professionals** such as stock brokers and advisors have lost some of their business to online trading websites like **e-Trade** and **robo-advisors** like

Betterment. **Robinhood** is a **free online** broker-age service that is subsequently stealing market share from traditional online brokers. Many banks are giving customers the ability to deposit checks via mobile apps or directly at ATMs, reducing the need for human bank tellers. Payment systems like **Apple Pay** and **PayPal** make even obtaining physical cash unnecessary.

- **Job recruiters** have been displaced by websites like **LinkedIn**, **Indeed.com**, and **Monster**, Print classified ads have also been replaced by these sites, while sites like Craigslist have replaced other kinds of classifieds.

- Uber, Lyft, and other car-sharing apps are giving **traditional taxi and livery companies** a run for their money.

- **Airbnb** and **HomeAway** are doing the same for the **hotel and motel industry**.

- Driverless cars, such as those being developed by **Google** may prove to replace all sorts of **driving jobs,** including bus and truck drivers, taxi drivers, and chauffeurs.

- Drone technology may revolutionize **the way products are delivered**, and Amazon is trying to make that a reality. Drones may also replace pilots in a number of specializations including those pilots in the film, crop-dusting, traffic monitoring, and law enforcement sectors. For years, fighter pilots have been replaced by drones on numerous military missions.

- 3D printing is growing rapidly, and the technology is becoming better and faster. In a few years, it may be possible to manufacture a wide variety of goods on demand and at home. This will disrupt the **manufacturing industry** and diminish the importance of logistics and inventory management. Goods will no longer have to be transported overseas. Assembly line workers have already been largely displaced by industrial robots.

- **Postal workers** first saw bad news with the widespread use of email reducing the volume of everyday mail. High-tech mail sorting machines will eliminate even more jobs in the postal service.

- **Fast food workers** recently protested to raise the minimum wage. Fast food companies responded by investing in computerized kiosks which can take orders without the need for humans. **Retail cashiers** have also been displaced at supermarkets and big box stores with self-checkout lines. Toll-booth attendants have been replaced by systems like **EZPass.**

- **Radio DJs** are largely a thing of the past. Software now chooses most of the music played, inserts ads, and even reads the news.

- Educational sites such as Khan Academy and Udemy, as well as Massively Open Online Courses offered by leading universities for free, will greatly reduce the need for **teachers and college professors** over time. It is plausible that children today will receive their undergraduate education largely online and at very little cost.

- **Traditional television distribution** is being upended by digital distribution outlets such as **NetFlix** and **Hulu.** People are dropping their cable or satellite TV services opting to stream online instead. **Spotify** and **iTunes** have done the same for the recording industry: people now choose to download or stream on demand rather than buy records or CDs.

- **Libraries** and librarians are moving online. References like Wikipedia have replaced the multi-volume encyclopedia. Librarians used to help people find information and conduct research, but much of that can be done individually over the internet nowadays.

- **Farmers and ranchers** used to make up over 50% of the U.S. workforce. Today less than 2.5% are employed in this sector. Yet, more food than ever is being produced in America due to the automation in agriculture and food production.

## The Bottom Line

While many industries and jobs will be lost to technological advancement, it remains to be seen whether there will be new jobs created that can be filled by those who lose their jobs. The problem today is that many of the jobs being replaced by technology are not inherently technological – and therefore those workers may not have the proper technological skills needed. It will be those individuals who can interface with technology who are likely to succeed – those with computer programming skills will be more richly rewarded than those who can accomplish physical labor. This next wave of creative destruction may, in fact, bring more destruction than creation.

And so while technology has changed industries forever, there is desire by many entrepreneurs today to get back to a "simpler time" when craftsman worked with their hands and made something useful. Artist, woodworkers, musicians, writers, carpenters, actors, real estate home flippers, voice over talent, and a host of hundreds of these kinds of businesses are springing up all around the world in a new almost 'back-to-basics revolution." A simpler life is becoming more attractive. The commute for hours on the highways will always be there for some, but creating the **perfect lifestyle** for yourself is what more and more of us are striving for.

This is a very special and unique moment in time, where creating and building a business can be something truly special. Commit to it. Learn all that you can. Make it real. Do something today to forward your dream. Research. Take classes if you need to. There is a movement towards that "perfect lifestyle." So be a part of it. It's an amazing opportunity to see what's in you and what you can accomplish with focus and a resolves to do something magical.

To your success always. ~Bob

# How to Use This Book

Anyone can pick up a book, but not everyone will read it, so find the nuggets in it and apply those lessons by applying them to real life situations. Did you know that of a 100 books purchased that only 5% of readers get past the first chapter and table of contents? Wow! Successful business owners are people who follow through.

The difference between a person who uses this book to quickly set in motion and create their new business and the one who simply reads it and says wow that was cool and puts it down, is ACTION.

To get the most from this Business Idea book you have to do three things:

1. **Read it.** It's a pretty quick read and **be open** to accepting new ideas as you read. Study with the notion of finding something you really need.
2. **Take Notes.** Apply any ideas about the marketing, which ideas have promise, which ones you could really see yourself doing.
3. **Take action** and begin to implement what you need to do to create your new business. This is always where the

rubber meets the road. Remember, creating a business is fairly easy, but creating the "perfect lifestyle while creating your business, is the goal."

This book has been designed and written in a *free-flowing" format on purpose without a division of topics* by header, i.e. craft businesses, technology, gardening, new product development, etc. I wanted you to look and read through it, with a *"stream of consciousness approach."* Highlight those ideas in the book that "ring true for you" or that simply "sound an alarm" within you and then sort through them later and decide which ones to research and explore further.

So of course, you can't skim a book and expect the book to do the work for you. Your results will depend on how much action you take, research you do and time you invest in it. Joe Vitale once said, *"money loves speed."* Taking what inspiration you have and doing something with it, quickly, is the key. Even if you discard an idea, do it quickly. Remember though, that the goal is to find the right business venture so you can begin it quickly. Enthusiasm for your business idea is rocket fuel. Use that enthusiasm to fuel your ideas, research, develop a business plan and see your business idea for what it is and can be.

It will be tempting to procrastinate until tomorrow when you have more time. We all do it. But when starting a business, your time invested early on in the formation of the idea needs to be acted upon. Ask yourself this question after deciding on a business idea..."will I be more or less likely to work on this tomorrow?"

While managing your time is important, managing your energy, enthusiasm and motivation are crucial in the early phase of your new venture. Will this venture inspire you tomorrow? If you can't get a business idea out of your mind, dream about it while you sleep or run it over in your mind constantly while showering or commuting to work, you likely have a workable business, that in your mind's eye, you can see yourself doing. It sings to your heart. It screams in your ears and moves you to action. So now we have it. That's what we want. A business idea that moves us. Now do it!

# Why Start A Business?

Let me ask you a serious question. Have you ever dreamed of really owning your own business? Maybe you're running a business now? Or maybe you'd like to try something new? Or heck, maybe you'd like a larger paycheck? Right? :-) That's okay. It's my intent that this book will create some ideas and options for you. This book is **not** meant to be a detailed "how-to-get-started" in a certain business type of book, but rather designed to spark an idea in your mind where you can then dig-down deeper and discover what your business passion is and what the ideal business for you will look like. There are plenty of "start-up" books out there.

When you start and operate your own successful business it doesn't matter where you've come from or even what your background is.

- Most businesses don't need a lot of capital to invest.

- You don't need a college degree.

- You don't need to be "tech savvy" or great with computers.

- Whether you're an engineer, a restaurant chef, or a welder you can create your own business and make money with it.

And the best part is ...

Most of these businesses are easy to begin and scalable for growth and expansion... which means that you can quickly double, triple, or even quadruple your income just by "turning it up."

Imagine ...

1. doing what you want when you want to do it

2. living life by your own rules

3. traveling all over the world

4. buying nice things for yourself and your loved ones

5. creating income at will and having the time to enjoy it

When you begin your own business, the best part is, that you'll be your own boss. You'll have freedom, security and peace of mind and "money worries" will be a thing of the past (as the business takes off). But not always at first either, as start-ups take a little time. You'll turn the corner pretty quickly if your business is well planned and you work your tail off to market it properly.

So, do you have a million dollar business idea that you'd like to pursue right now? Fantastic! And odds are that you've been thinking about it for some time. If not, then please read through these ideas and highlight them. Maybe your business begins with a simple idea that you then can build into something financially rewarding. Maybe you begin from home, or maybe you'll need a sizeable business loan to go all-in and create something completely new and revolutionary. Sometimes businesses are created with a Kickstarter loan where others fund your business creation. (Check out **https://www.kickstarter.com/start)**.If you're looking at funding for your venture, consider these online funding platforms. They can be a great way to realize your business dreams.

Let me congratulate you too, on taking the first important step to entrepreneurship and business ownership. It's not always easy, but generally it's worth it. Let me reassure you that you'll be just fine. You can do it! With a little research, a little start-up capital, and a commitment to your businesses success, you'll experience the benefits of business ownership very soon. You just have to begin. So as Stephen Covey has said, "begin with the end in mind". What can you see yourself doing that can make a great income for you and your family and makes a difference in the lives of your customers? It all starts with an idea.

There are many benefits to owning your own business. Let me reiterate just one more time why owning a successful business can be fun and create the lifestyle you desire...

- You're the BOSS! No one can tell you what to do and when. (You may be your toughest boss ever though so be kind to yourself please).

- You can truly be paid what you're worth. This is your chance to really shine and earn the income you deserve.

- You create your work schedule and make all the rules for your business.

- Almost every expense is a tax deduction. Get with your accountant at the beginning of your start-up and have them set you up and get you started right.

- You'll have the freedom to do what you want and when you want to do it. Of course your business will have its own demands on your time. But you choose.

- No more major commute. If you work from home in your new venture, your office may be across the hallway.

- You'll have less stress, believe it or not. Less stress may translate into better overall health.

- You'll be able to exercise and work out anytime during your day too.

- You can spend more quality time with your family and friends.

- Your business is a separate entity and can develop its own credit.

- The prestige of being a successful business owner is exhilarating and rewarding.

# Why This Book Now?

Small business has become BIG business and there has never been a better, easier time to begin a new venture than now. And by the way, most businesses in this book don't need much money to start. Sure, it's nice to have money to invest in yourself and your company. But if you think about starting your business in small steps and sticking to the philosophy of "Do what you can with what you've got" – you will be able to follow that dream and find success.

Here are *16 Surprising Statistics About Small Businesses* that John Nazar, entrepreneurship writer wrote for Forbes magazine in September of 2013. It's pretty amazing.

- The SBA defines a small business as an enterprise having **fewer than 500 employees**
- There are almost **28 million small businesses** in the US and over 22 million are self-employed with no additional payroll or employees (these are called non-employers)
- **Over 50%** of the working population (120 million individuals) **works in a small business**
- Small businesses have generated over **65% of the net new jobs** since 1995

- Approximately **543,000 new businesses** get started **each month** (but more employer businesses shut down than start up each month)

- 7 out of 10 new employer **firms survive** at least 2 years, **half at least 5 years**, a third at least 10 years and a quarter stay in business 15 years or more

- **52%** of all small businesses are **home-based**

- There were **22.5 million non-employer firms** in 2011 (up almost 2% from the year before)

- To classify as a **"non-employer"** business you must have annual **business receipts of $1,000** or more and be subject to federal income taxes

- Approximately **75% of all U.S. businesses are non-employer** businesses

- 19.4 million non-employer businesses are **sole proprietorships**, 1.6 million are **partnerships** and 1.4 million are **corporations**

- The **fastest growing sector** for freelance businesses in 2011 included **auto repair shops, beauty salons and dry cleaners**

- Total **revenues** from **non-employers** hit **$989.6 billion** in 2011 (up 4.1% from 2010)

- Non-employers had **average revenues of $44,000**

- Around **80%** of non-employer businesses for 2011 (or 18 million businesses) reported **less than $50,000 in receipts**

## Sources:

United States Census Bureau. "2011 Non-employer Statistics. U.S.-Dept. of Commerce

http://censtats.census.gov/cgi-bin/nonemployer/nonsect.pl

Small Business Administration Office of Advocacy

http://www.sba.gov/sites/default/files/FAQ_Sept_2012.pdf

United States Census Bureau: Statistics about Business Size (including Small Business

http://www.census.gov/econ/smallbus.html

One thing is for sure, as a small business owner you are not alone! In the most recent www.sba.gov trends in small business we find that:

There are millions of small businesses across the United States traveling the same road as you each and every day. Although your business operates in its own unique fashion, the cumulative impact of the small business sector is enormous. You are part of an amazing trend in America.

# Small Business is BIG Business!

- Today, there are over 28+ million small businesses in America and account for 54% of all U.S. sales.

- Small businesses provide 55% of all jobs and 66% of all net new jobs since the 1970s.

- The 600,000 plus franchised small businesses in the U.S. account for 40% of all retail sales and provide jobs for some 8 million people.

- The small business sector in America occupies 30-50% of all commercial space, an estimated 20-34 billion square feet.

Furthermore, the small business sector is growing rapidly. While corporate America has been "downsizing" for some time, the rate of small business "start-ups" has grown, and the rate for small business failures has declined.

- The number of small businesses in the United States has increased 49% since 1982.

- Since 1990, as big business eliminated 4 million jobs, small businesses added 8 million new jobs.

For more interesting facts about the Small Businesses community visit:

- <u>U.S. Census Bureau's Statistics of U.S. Businesses</u>

- <u>SBA Office of Advocacy's Firm Size Data</u>

- <u>DOE's Energy Information Administration</u>

- <u>National Small Business Association</u>

There are so many benefits to being a small business owner and entrepreneur today. It's my hope that as you search through these 1001 business ideas featuring, craft and talent businesses, technology, farming, sales and marketing companies, and current top job ideas that you will create for yourself a new career outlook.

It's important to note also that every business sector has a market leader. They are a great source of tips, tricks and information. You'll learn from observing the best companies in the business sector you are looking at. Use the experiences of other successful companies where you can, and keep yourself from trying to re-invent the proverbial wheel. Business and industry newsletters and Google searches will also yield you up-to-date market trends and business news. Use this information to plot your course.

If your business is totally unique and different, that's awesome. However, there will still be some basic metrics to follow where sales, marketing, advertising, compliance, basic business principles and human resources are concerned. Learn quickly from the industry leaders and improve on the ideas you've gained. I've listed some small business resources and sites that may be helpful to you as well at the end of the book.

So, are you ready? I you purchased the book get a pen, a bookmark so you know where you've left off and a yellow highlighter. If you got the e-book version, have a notebook and pen ready to write down the business numbers that move you. You may also want to write down your first impressions of the ones you like. Your impressions count. This is the enthusiasm you'll need to move your business forward.

Treat this as an assignment. Read it all the way through. Even if you only skim it the first time, go through it at least twice. You will see it much differently the second time. You'll gain new insights. The old adage is that you can't put your foot in the same river twice, is true when reading book like this.

Certain business ideas will come back to you, hours, even days later. It's as if your subconscious mind is sorting each one and confirming to your mind that this business idea will work if your choose it. Your intuition and business sense need to work together here. As they do, you'll get the value of having over a thousand workable ideas that can create the perfect lifestyle for you.

Remember, skim the book the first time and then read it thoroughly through the second time. Ready? So let's get started then shall we?

# 1001 BUSINESS IDEAS

Finding the Right Business to Fuel Your Passion and Create Your Perfect Lifestyle

1. **Become an Event Planner.** One of the first things you need to do is visit every potential event location with which you plan to work. Work with the marketing manager to tour each site and learn what is available at each location. Start a database that will allow you to sort venues by varying features--the number of people each site holds, if there is AV equipment available on site, will you need to arrange for rental chairs, etc. Then when you are beginning to plan an event with a client, you can find out what the key parameters are for the event and easily pull up the three or four sites that meet the basic criteria, and engagement parties, etc.

2. **Become an Expert Witness**. One way to make money in this field is by being an expert witness yourself. If you have an expertise that could be useful in legal cases, you can market yourself to attorneys to act as an expert witness.

For example, a neurologists would be an excellent witness because of their knowledge of head trauma and nerve damage as in a car accident. Another way to be active in the expert witness field is to play a sort of matchmaker, matching attorneys up with expert witnesses for their cases--either for the defense or for the prosecution. Expert witnesses for big money cases can be expected to fly anywhere to testify. There's no reason your database of witnesses can't be from all parts of the country.

3. **Film Making Course.** Put together a home study course about the technical aspects of film making. This course might be the cornerstone of your own online or main street film school. Sell from ads in film magazines, Craigslist and free online classified ad sites.

4. **Learn to invest in crypto-currencies.** You've probably heard of Bitcoin, but did you know that there are nearly 1600 other crypto-currencies that are trading throughout the world? Check out https://coinmarketcap.com/1. As of this writing (and it changes hourly) the market capitalization rate is over $335 billion and climbing for cryto-currencies.

Real money is being invested and made in this arena and sometimes at 10,000% ROI over a few months. Maybe it's time to get check this out after all. Perhaps start a CC club where you live or online with friends and explore what the best digital currencies to invest in. A small investment may yield a nice ROI. Like any investment, be informed or be prepared to lose your investment.

5. **Set yourself up in business as a music concert promoter**. Approach a local pop or rock group and offer to organize a gig for them. If your first gig is successful slowly work your way up in the concert promoting business. Apply your knowledge from the agent/group management course.

6. **Facebook or YouTube Fan Page Development**. Start a service that produces content for Facebook and YouTube Fan Pages. This can be for pop group fan clubs, businesses, celebrities and personalities and political candidates too. Sell your service to the groups and monetize it through the fans. An important part of this business is that it gives a lot of scope for the selling of advertising space too. YouTube videos, depending on the number of viewers, pays you for ad clicks too. So build up your following (subscriptions) by asking everyone who visits your YouTube channel to like and subscribe.

7. **Car Washing & Polishing & Detail Work**. If you live in a busy road and you are at home all day, place a good looking sign outside you house stating that you do car washing and polishing. Put a 10'x10'canopy in the driveway with a banner and prices and watch the world beat a path to your door with the quality work that you do. Also advertise that you give a personal service and that car owners can call at your house any time. Craigslist and other free classified sites are cheap and effective places to start, but A-frame signs at your business will also pull very effectively too.

8. **Cook Books.** Bring out a correspondence course about how to write cook books. The course might include information about: How to devise recipes, how to present them in written form and what makes a successful cookery book. Produce a prospectus and advertise in women's magazines.

9. **Create and Operate an Etsy or Shopify store**. Sell your crafts and treasures there. Etsy and Shopify both have a way to process your payments and sales taxes and take names and addresses so you can send your client their merchandise. Both are free to sign up. Visit their websites. Shopify has additional features that they charge you for so there's a monthly fee, but well worth it and part of the cost of doing business. Visit YouTube for success stories and training as well.

10. **Become a midwife and labor coach.** Becoming a midwife can help a birthing mother in any labor environment, from a hospital to a midwife clinic to home. Midwives or doulas, are non-medical professionals who offer information, emotional support, and physical assistance in the process of giving birth. While licensing for midwives is not required by most states, getting certified by **DONA International**, the only certifying body for this profession, is a good idea. Midwives do have to deal with unpredictable schedules, but they easily can do this work from home. Midwives generally charge between $500 and $1000 per birth.

11. **Power Washing Business.** Start a service which cleans wire baskets and supermarket carts. Baskets and carts often spend most of the day on a dusty floor or outside, open to the elements with human hands all of them. Power washing can also be done in front of every store front business in your area. Use flyers and call managers and owners to get new business. Offer to do this in the early morning before the business opens. Research pricing in your area of other competitors, if there are any, and see what they charge. Be competitive.

12. **Create a mail or online business which specializes in selling products which help people sleep.** Products might include: Sleep inducing CD's or MP3's, special bedtime clothing, herbal pillows, books and guides on how to sleep better.

13. **Paint on wood stylistic house numbers and names.** These painted numbers and names will be an attractive alternative to the traditional names burned into sliced logs. Get your work stocked at shops which sell garden products or household goods.

14. **Phone App Development.** If you know your way around an app, consider designing one and cashing in. This can even be a form of passive income that pays you forever. One man earns over **$6,000 per month** from the Bible app he created. Want to learn? **Https://www.codewithchris.com** and then **https://www.chupamobile.com**. Creating an app isn't hard once you have an idea on how it can solve a customer problem. Believe me, there's always someone who can help you develop your concept and the app for you. Fun and definitely an up-and-coming industry.

15. **Drive for Uber and/or Lyft and be paid well for it.** Go to their websites and sign-up today. Don't have a car? Uber and Lyft will buy you one them on a contract with them over time. Drivers in large metropolitan cities earn $60 to $100k a year for fulltime work. You set your own hours and work where you want to work. Smaller towns and less hours will result in less money too. Great side-gig and each passenger has already paid through their phone app. Very cool way to make money.

16. **Devise and produce a board game which simulates the experience of starting a business.** The usual problem of bringing out a board game is the difficulty of getting it stocked in shops. However, a game about internet marketing or staring a business can be sold via the internet today through social media and Amazon for example to business opportunity seekers and would be entrepreneurs or parents teaching their children how to be more business-minded.

17. **Ancestor and Family Tree Research**. Give one-on-one instruction to those actively seeking out their ancestors. With the explosion of information available online now very few know how and where to look for it. People today have many options for researching but are very confused on how and where to begin. You can also write a beginners book which teaches about how to trace your own ancestry and publish on Amazon & CreateSpace for your paperback publication. Genealogists depending on their skill level and complexity of the research they are doing, are paid $10-$25/hour or are paid by the assignment. Begin by checking this website out. **http://www.jobmonkey.com/uniquejobs4/genealogis t/.**This is great place to begin. Also at **FamilySearch.org** where literally billions of records can be accessed.

18. **Buy and sell oil paintings.** Buy new paintings from artists and old paintings from collectors and householders. Sell the paintings from: home, a roadside site, a stall at crafts fairs or hire stalls for exhibiting all the paintings you have for sale.

19. **Start a manufacturing business which is devoted to making doorstops.** These doorstops might range from the humble wooden wedge to the more exotic and unusual. Package them in polythene bags, staple on a printed card and get them stocked at gift shops.

20. **Decorate everyday objects with pressed flowers**. Add an inlaid design of pressed flowers to trays, coasters, jewelry boxes, paperweights, picture frames, wall-hangings, desk sets and table tops. Check out Etsy.com for ideas.

21. **Courier Service**. If you live in a bustling, high population centers, chances are businesses could use a local courier service. Unlike the big name services, you can offer more flexible pick-up and drop off times, which can be a godsend to many small businesses, like attorneys and legal services and mortgage companies. According to About.com, half of couriers earn in the $17,000 to $27,000 range. Couriers can be a valuable and efficient way to move important papers, contracts and legal documents across a city. Consider this if you have such desires.

22. **Make wooden Tick-Tack-Toe games**. Drill nine holes in a small square block and paint on a grid. Next make ten pegs and pint on each peg an 'O' or an 'X'. Place the grid and pegs into a clear bag and staple on a product card. Make these unique and fun.

23. **Brass Ornaments**. Bring together a range of brassware ornaments so you can have a table and display at crafts fairs, antique markets and car and boat shows.

24. **Ambitious & Clever.** Publish a newsletter which has the title "Ambitious Persons Way to Wealth" or "Clever People Don't Work Hard". The contents of your newsletter might be in a vein similar to Joe Karbo's "The Lazy Man's Way to Riches" published years ago.

25. **Create, set up and run school classes/courses on an area of expertise for which you are known.** Organize one-day or two-day seminars and also provide courses for those who would like to take up the career of doing what you're doing and provide hands-on coaching.

26. **Write and publish a manual about how to make money from property**. In the manual include chapters on: Buying, developing and selling land, buying properties for conversions or renovations for flipping for quick profits, commercial or multiunit investing or how to do lease to own property.

The market is always strong for this sort of information. Put a course or a book together and provide one on exclusive coaching.

27. **Organize and run an investment school**. Give tuition to solo students and to groups about different types of investments such as shares, gilt-edged securities, unit trusts, USM, antiques, stamps, arts, etc. For each area covered, prepare lesson plans and follow these closely.

28. **VIP KID** – This is one of the hottest ways to make up to $22.00/hour! The company is looking for online teachers. **https://t.vipkid.com.cn/opportunity** is a China based company that is looking to hire English speaking teachers to teach one-on-one Chinese students immersion in the basics. You don't have to speak Chinese but you should have a bachelor's degree in any discipline, a computer with camera capability and be willing to work 7.5 hours minimum a week. The perfect side-hustle. Work 2 hours and make $44.00. They are looking for teachers that are high-energy, great with children, and motivated to work with a promising company that is growing at a fast pace in China.

29. **Start a crafts business which uses interesting foreign coins to make Jewelry**. Incorporate coins into pendant bracelet, brooches, necklaces and earrings. Alternatively, make Jewelry which features re-production coins from the ancient world.

30. **Use small sea-shells strung together to make necklaces**. Find a trade source of small sea-shells and either set up your own production line or employ homeworkers.

31. **Produce drama DVD videos, CD's or MP3's.** Professional actors and actresses perform a play on video. However, there is one character missing from the video. This character is played by a viewer of the video. The viewer learns his or her part and becomes part of the play at home.

32. **Create a folder of sample sales letters for all occasions**. The letters might sell: advice, maintenance, products, a service which gives free quotes, etc. Sell these folders by direct mail to small businesses.

33. **Earn money by selling gold chain by the inch** at public events such as fairs, markets and exhibitions. This is still a popular booth. Watch your inventory though as the cost of gold has gone up dramatically since its business inception.

34. **Jewelry Making Supplies**. Put together your own catalog of Jewelry making supplies. Locate the wholesale sources of products by doing the routine work of researching online for best quality and pricing. Email potential suppliers and share with them your plans. Throughout the country there are thousands of craft workers who would welcome your new online catalog.

35. **Earn a living by buying gold and silver jewelry** from people who need instant cash. Because the client's need for cash now is greater than their desire to wait and get a little higher price, your mark-up can be very good. Only buy Jewelry which you know is real you can re-sell quickly for a profit. Test all gold and silver and platinum purity for before you purchase it. Test kits are cheap and will save you from mistakes. Pay cash to your clients and they will come back over and over again.

36. **Licensed practical and vocational nurse.** A real need for LVNs and RNs is on the rise again with healthcare needs for nursing at an all-time high. Care for patients in hospitals, clinics, nursing homes, and similar institutions is in high demand. Postsecondary non-degree award is needed. Median income is $42,490 in 2014.

37. **Prepare a mixture of dried herbs and aromatherapy oils for adding to bathwater.** Invent a brand name for your product like "(your surname) Original Bath Herbs". Package each mixture of herbs and get them stocked at various retailers and sell online.

38. **Software and App Development**. Bring out a selection of computer programs which can be sold as a business opportunity.

For example, one program might be for starting a computerized dating agency, another for writing a newsletter or classified ad sheet, a third for starting a computerized marketplace. Get creative here. App and software development are two of the hottest industries today.

39. **Make leather and wooden souvenir luggage tags.** These tags might feature the name of a holiday town and a popular scene. Personalize for an add-on sale. Get your tags stocked at shops visited by tourists.

40. **A-Frame Street Signs**. Many businesses benefit from having an A-frame street sign on a busy street in front of their business. Why? Top of mind, in your face advertising always draws eyes and in drive-time can be very effective. One chiropractor used an A-frame sign out front and his A-Frame signs contributed $30,000 in revenues for the 4 days each week he was open that year. Both the A-Frame and Two of the 24" x 36" full color coroplast signs can be purchased on EBay for example, for as low as $125-$150. You'll also need a bike lock ($15) to secure them to poles too. These can easily be sold to local businesses for $250-$300. When you are the *"go-to sign guy" in* your town, when business people need a sign or banner, they'll just call you. Brand your business! Setup your website and drive traffic to it too. Also you must distribute flyers (or glossy 5" x 8") postcards front and back, to every business in your area. You'll never look back.

41. **Arrange Music & Lyrics**. Start a service which arranges for people to have their original pop lyrics set to music. This service is to satisfy the vanity of lyricists. Offer clients a complete, low cost package. Attract custom by placing ads in the music press.

42. **Devise quizzes which test and improve a person's vocabulary**. Sell these to a magazine or newspaper on a regular basis. Alternatively you might do quizzes which test a person's knowledge of a regional dialect. Sell these to regional papers or magazines.

43. **Unwanted Furniture.** Call door-to-door and offer to buy unwanted furniture. Offer free pickup with your tuck. Use local media to advertise your interest in buying second-hand furniture. Sell what you buy from free ads in local papers, or start your own second-hand furniture shop.

44. **Personal Stylist-Shopper**. If you have an eye for clothes and know what styles look best on what body types, this could be for you. So turn your passion for fashion into a business by becoming a personal stylist/shopper. You'll feel good about making others look great too.

45. **Start an enterprise which reproduces classic poems on postcards and posters.** Also do framed prints of classic poems. Sell these from a stall in an antiques or crafts market or get them stocked at souvenir or gift shops.

46. **Create a local town Monopoly game**. Approach all local stores, vendors, manufacturers and city offices and get their name on various squares of the game. You charge a fee for their advertising on the game board. Collect money in advance. Create a certain number of game you will produce and sell the games for $25 each. With 1000 games produced you make $25,000 plus ad fees minus the cost of game production. You should net $20,000 on a 1000 games. Can you do this in several communities and cities? Of course. This could be lucrative.

47. **Business Trade Publication**. Publish a monthly audio CD/MP3 from one trade, such as newsagents, grocers, hair salons, booksellers, etc. Each audio should give: Trade news, management tips, suggestions for improving sales, etc. Organize a direct mail campaign to recruit subscribers, website development and new client acquisition techniques.

48. **Roadside Fruit Stand**. In season sales of strawberries, oranges, bags of nuts and watermelons are a fun stop for drivers wanting to get a great deal on products they typically buy at a Farmer's Market. Hit the busy intersections. Weekends are best and local authorities aren't patrolling for licensing.

**49. Short Story Development**. Bring out a correspondence course about how to write short stories for profit. Create a book and market it through Amazon. There are many aspiring authors looking to break into the writing profession. Short stories is where many folks like to begin.

**50. Poetry Writing.** Produce a correspondence course about how to write good poetry. If most poets received a small amount of money from their works as they go, they can sustain their writing for a longer period, and their work would improve dramatically. Sell your poetry course by advertising in literary and women's magazines and your book on poetry through the world's largest bookstore, Amazon.

**51. Begin a business which deals in old and new American comics**. This business might: 1) Sell comics from an online catalog. 2) Operate a comics of the month club for specialized collectors and 3) Run a comic's business at fairs and markets and Comic-cons.

**52. Write to overseas publishers of English language newsletters and offer to act as the distributor for their newsletter in this country.** In your letter to the publishers outline the benefits they will gain if they let you distribute their newsletter. Take an affiliate fee or a percentage of the price.

53. **Paint attractive art on rocks to make souvenir paperweights and doorstops.** The art might take the form of abstract pattern, traditional pictures or tourist scenery. Call your rocks "designer rocks". Add a rubber base to paperweights and a rubber edge to doorstops.

54. **Make wooden jigsaw puzzles**. Make puzzles for pre-school children. As an add-on, make jigsaw puzzle jewelry or earrings. Call your goods jigsaw puzzle Jewelry. Sell from a booth at fairs, car and boat shows or get it stocked at trendy shops. Open your own website and market your own good jewelry from there. Etsy is another place to go market your handmade goods.

55. **Metal Art.** Take metal rods and tubes of different diameters and cut into slices. Arrange the slices to make pictures and patterns. Braze them as needed. Mount these pictures and sell as craftwork. Or produce kits for making pictures with slices of rods and tubes. Use mail or online to sell these kits to craft workers and those that appreciate your handiwork.

56. **Business Development**. Write and sell articles or books about starting a business and making money. Sell the manuscripts to publishers of business opportunity books, newsletters, magazines and newspapers. Market also on Amazon.

57. **Nursery Rhymes.** Set up a business which produces a quality audio CD/MP3 library of nursery rhymes. Sell these by either getting them stocked in bookshops or by starting a monthly club. Sell on iTunes that is a media player, media library of audiobooks, poems, music, Internet radio broadcast podcasts, and mobile device management application developed by Apple Inc. Google Play and Amazon have similar platforms from which to sell also. Uploading should be easy and you receive a commission for every download.

58. **Poetry Directory & Competition**. Compile and publish a monthly bulletin which informs subscribers of poetry competitions they are eligible to enter at home and abroad. Target your recruitment campaign for subscribers at practicing poets.

59. **Bring out a series of plans for woodworkers, soft toy makers, leather workers and other craft workers.** Either sell printed copies of these plans at wholesale prices or sell the reproduction rights. Then any Craft worker or hobbyist can start a mail or online business selling the plans.

60. **Publish a Who's Who Book of Network Marketers every year.** This could be the Top 500 MLM'ers from all over of the world.

Networkers pay to be in the book or to be featured in the book. This is an online E-Book through Amazon or can be a printed copy through CreateSpace or Lulu.com. Highlight the success stories of networkers from various companies. Use the website to sell your books, products, affiliate offers and subscriptions to various networking groups and events. MLM has become a $200 billion dollar a year industry and is growing rapidly, as the entry level is much lower than a franchise. Normally $200 to $1000 to be involved.

61. **Begin an enterprise which makes model paper products for dolls and dolls' houses**. These might include: Newspapers, money, stationery, napkins, paper hats, Christmas cards, etc. Sell these products by mail or online to doll makers and collectors.

62. **Write a non-fiction book which may, for example, be about your favorite hobby**. Enlist a book printer to produce copies of the book. (Check out **www.lulu.com** or **www.createspace.com**. Sell these to the market that would be interested in the contents. You might, for example, place ads in hobby magazines or on Craigslist. If a non-fiction book, for example on a health concern that you've thoroughly researched, promote it through Amazon's **www.kdp.amazon.com** program and create an ebook that you can profit from while delivering your book's information to thousands.

63. **Reading & Writing English.** Give personal lessons in your own home (or place of business) on how to read and write good English. Advertise your service by placing cards in windows of local newsstands. Point out the advantages of taking the course, such as getting a better job and helping the children with their homework, etc. Use Craigslist and free sites that can get you many eye balls on your ads. Create the ads in Spanish too so those that want to speak and write better English can read the ad copy.

64. **Start a singles contact magazine or website for your area**. Each post might include both small ads from people looking for partners and editorials of interest to single people. Use press and magazine advertising to build up a list of subscribers.

65. **Set up a holiday companion introduction service**. Your service matches and introduces single people who do not have anyone to go on holiday with. Place classified ads in numerous publications to attract clients. Or produce a publication which lists people who are looking for holiday companions.

66. **Business Consulting Business.** Write and publish blog posts and do podcast for those who want to start a successful business.

The newsletter might, for example, discuss effective ways of: Selling, managing, generating ideas, locating suppliers and finding customers. Use your local library service to research these topics and get the word out by direct mail and phone calls. Secure clients by helping them in the startup and organization of their business.

67. **Wire Ornaments & Wire Wrapping Jewelry**. Begin a crafts enterprise which turns out wire craft ornaments and wire wrapped jewelry. These ornaments are free-standing, 3-D objects which consist entirely of wire: the wire makes the outlines. The ornaments might be in the shape of: Christmas decorations, airplanes, helicopters, people, animals, boats or bicycles. The wire wrapped jewelry is typically learned online and takes gemstones and beautiful centerpiece quality topaz, crystals, etc. and wraps the jewelry to be work earrings and necklaces. Handmade jewelry is more expensive because of the labor involved. Go to Etsy.com to sell yours and see what others have done.

68. **Start a Catering Business.** If you love to cook on a grand scale, why not start a catering business out of your home? How much you make depends on the scale of the assignments you take, and your ability to correctly decide how much your materials will cost. But this is also an industry where you can start small and work your way up to bigger gigs—and profits. Weddings, birthdays, receptions, business

luncheons and banquets are where you'll want to focus. It's where the biggest money is and are likely to get referrals for your next catering event.

69. **Furniture Refinishing and Repair.** You might have made a hobby of refinishing and repairing garage sale finds. Now, put your skills to work profitably by offering to make old furniture as good as new. After all, retro is definitely in these days.

70. **Produce a series of storytelling videos**. An actor or actress reads classic novels directly to the camera. Hire out these videos by post. You can use whole or part of classic stories for which the copyright has expired. This is the case for any work where the writer has been dead for 50 or more years. Also incorporate bedtime stories for children.

71. **Coastal Boat Trips**. Start a venture which organizes river or coastal boat trips for: Business parties, wedding receptions, anniversaries, birthday parties, etc. Your service would do things like: Organize transportation to the boat, booking catering services, hiring entertainers, speakers and hosts or hostesses.

72. **Musical Background**. If you can play a musical instrument, earn money by providing background music at: Restaurants, wine bars, tea-rooms, hotel breakfasts, amusement arcades, or ice or roller skating rinks.

Also play during the interval at theatres and/or cinemas.

73. **Sell copies of theatrical plays by Mail or website.** Put together a wide range of new and second-hand publications and produce a catalog. Advertise your catalog in both the theatre press and theatre programs. Make your selection High School friendly too, as many small high schools drama teachers like being able to have a selection of great plays that their students can perform.

74. **CD's & DVD's.** Buy and sell CD's (compact disks) and DVD's (Digital Versatile Disk). Buy collections of disks from Craigslist and EBay in bulk, and then use local ads to find buyers in your area. The disks you buy can be sold via mail, from a flea market booth, or your online store. Music stores are struggling to stay open these days. You may be provide a real service in your city with high quality second-hand disks. The world is streaming now. CD's and DVD's will not make a dramatic comeback, but they are great to have in your entertainment library too.

75. **Fashionable Clothing.** Have a booth which sells fashionable clothes somewhere in your community. Fashionable clothing rarely goes out of style. Know the industry and what is hot. Your booth might be a full-time business, working at street fairs, flea markets or it may be part-time and appear at craft and antique fairs.

76. **Set up a sheet music of the month club.** Each month send members a selection of sheets to include the latest popular songs. Club members will include: Musicians, who play at clubs and pubs, record companies and keen amateur musicians.

77. **Sell Beatles or Elvis memorabilia by mail or from your online store.** Conduct your own research to discover what memorabilia you can produce yourself, for example, reprint photographs and duplicate press cuttings. Also buy goods from collectors and trade sources at home and abroad. Pick a popular musician and promote their work. T-shirts, etc.

78. **Children's Educational Audios.** Put together a mail or online catalog of children's educational audio CD's or MP3's. These might cover subjects such as spelling, reading and grammar rules, geography, history, etc. Produce some of the CD's or MP3's yourself and buy others from audio publishers.

79. **Do your own research to discover the secrets of conjuring.** Write a book about your findings and publish it yourself on Amazon and CreateSpace. The novel and sensational nature of this book, in a world of Harry Potter, will ensure that it sells well from ads in newspapers, social media and magazines.

80. **Write and record personalized songs.** Produce songs for all occasions, such as engagements, weddings, birthdays, anniversaries, births, homecomings and congratulations. Use classified ads in the personal columns to attract orders.

81. **Start a crafts business which produces gift tags decorated with pressed flowers**. Also do similar products like pressed flowers bookmarks. To make a bookmarker tape take two strips of clear 35mm film, place pressed flowers between the strips and tie the sprocket holes together with cotton.

82. **Stay At Home and Off-Hours Daycare Providers**. This is an especially good idea for stay-at-home-parents who need to bring in some money. You're already staying home with your kids: why not invite a few others to the party? Licensing for in-home day care varies from state to state, but you will want to make sure you comply with your local regulations. Median salary: $19,300. Though this is basically the same as above, it does deserve its own description. Finding someone to regularly watch children during off-hours, like second shift, weekends, or very early mornings, can be extremely difficult for parents. Offering care during off-peak hours means that you can command a higher fee.

**83. Open your own school of rock**. Provide classes about different aspects of rock, such as singing, playing electric guitars, writing music and songs, designing stage presentations, marketing and getting gigs, etc. Add credibility to the school by paying established rock musicians to give many of the lessons.

**84. Drum and Percussion Instruction**. Devise and produce an audio CD/MP3 course about how to play the drums and other percussion instruments. Use ads in the music press to sell this course. And/or get the course stocked at music shops.

**85. Produce kits for girls to make bead necklaces**. Package each kit in a small polythene bag and staple on a printed card. Mount these kits on a rack and get them displayed wherever you can. Styles change quickly and necklaces are age specific, so find out what teens are wearing today.

**86. Baby Sling**. Design your own brand of baby sling. Buy one of each of the baby slings currently on sale. Study them, reverse engineer them and develop one which is a composite of the best features. Manufacture and package them. Find appropriate retailers and wholesalers to stock them.

**87. Make charming and attractive quilts for babies and children.** Make the kind of quilts you would like your baby or child to have. Give your imagination free reign to see what ideas and designs you come up with. When you have finalized a design, go into business for yourself and start producing them. Hire others willing to work on a piece by piece basis, based on what you can get for them.

**88. Turn out knitwear and clothing for children.** Sell the garments from your own booth or through retailers. Open an Etsy store and begin selling your garments there. Make only the softest and highest quality you can. Your customers will really appreciate it and recommend you to their friends and expectant mothers.

**89. Start a Cricket Farm.** Not afraid of things that hop, crawl and go chirp in the night? You could try cricket farming. Stick with me here. It's pretty easy to get started, and there's actually more demand for crickets than you might think. Reptile owners have a need for their pets. You basically just need a large fish tank, egg cartons and dirt to set up your habitat, and once you start breeding the crickets, they can sell for up to $12 for 250.

By the way, the females lay five to 10 eggs... per day. There are free .pdf guides online to get your cricket farm started. Reptile owners have to feed their pets.

90. **Real World Experience Book**. Start a mail or online business which sells books, booklets and audio CD's or MP3's about how to deal with "real world experiences." Topics covered might include: Domestic violence in the home, break up of a marriage, death of a partner or child, being left at the marriage alter or failing your college exam. Life lessons and how to deal with them.

91. **Dog Massages.** Don't laugh, dogs love massages and dog lovers want their doggies to feel relaxed and loved too. You're your best friend a massage and a 20-minute spa day. If you adore animals and have strong hands, consider becoming a pet massage therapist. You could earn up to $105 an hour with three massages at $35 each.

92. **Create Men's Ties.** Bring out a selection of business and souvenir ties. The ties might feature the name or emblem of a holiday resort. Mount the ties on racks and get them displayed in shops which sell men's clothing. Brand it also, so your customers can come back and ask for them by name.

93. **Bring out your own range of shawls**. Increase the value of your shawls by giving each design a catchy name. Sell the shawls by mail or online or get them stocked at retailers.

94. **Ribbon Art.** Use ribbon to make souvenir pictures, for example: yellow ribbon can be used as the beach, blue as the sea, brown and green for palm trees, etc. Or design and produce kits for hobbyists. Sell by mail or online or through craft shops.

95. **Make Custom Banners.** Create business banner-signs for local companies who are running special sales, now hiring, and about the products or services those businesses sell. These banner can be made for about a $1.00-$1.50 per square foot from places like EBay and resold to customers for $4.00-$6.00 a square foot. This is called "triage" or being the middle man in a transaction. For example a 2' x 6' banner in full color with metal grommets for hanging the sign, would cost you a maximum of $18.00 and could be sold for $108.00 or a $90.00 profit. Triage works. Find other business applications for this too.

96. **Self-Improvement Videos.** Produce a series of videos which have titles such as: 'How to give up smoking', 'How to relax', 'How to lose weight' and 'How to sleep soundly'. Sell these by direct mail to business people. Or try to get a leading chain store to distribute them on a national basis. Open your own website store and sell them there.

97. **Fabric Sales.** Have your own fabrics booth and sell ordinary fabrics, rolls of discontinued lines and remnants. Many fabric stores will sell them cheaply to you to make way for newer fabric designs.

98. **Alterations and Repairs.** Do alterations and repairs for dry cleaning services, men's wear shops, factories and offices. Visit these places and inform them of your services. Offer, for example, to collect the goods once or twice a week.

99. **Produce cardboard, sightseeing periscopes and sell them at public events.** Make them yourself. Arrange for the card to be printed and shaped. Assemble the periscopes and add two small mirrors. Recruit sales people to sell these periscopes along the route of the event.

100. **Start a knitting patterns of the month club.** Each month, members of your club automatically receive a selection of the latest knitting patterns. Members select the patterns they want and return the rest. Or compile a top 30 of patterns and send new entries to club members.

101. **Elder Care.** In most cases, work-from-home elder care workers will make daily house calls to their patients to help with anything from meal preparation, laundry cleaning, to bathing to minor home repairs. Having a sincere love for seniors is the primary requisite. Having a contractual arrangement on hours, duties and wages is the next important

step to begin. Research your area's licensing, if any, and check around to see what other elder care individuals are charging.

102. **Start a home-based computer bureau.** There are hundreds of business computer programs available such as payroll programs record keeping for small businesses and taxes and accounting. Buy and use these programs to provide a computer service to local businesses.

103. **Lampshade Business.** Set up a business which promotes the making and matching of lampshades. Lampshade making can be sold as either an interesting hobby or a business opportunity. Produce a mail or online catalog of lampshade making equipment and supplies. Advertise your catalog in crafts magazines.

104. **Begin a web-based dating service.** Operate this service like a traditional dating service but, hold all your records on your secure server. Use the computer to aid your search for compatible partners. Have leaflets printed and place them in shops and advertise your service in the personal messages section of your local newspapers and everywhere you can online.

105. **Be a sleep consultant.** Large numbers of people have difficulty in sleeping at night. This is not usually a medical problem but can be corrected by using a suitable method or

attitude of mind. Provide people in your area with confidential advice about how to sleep soundly.

106. **Party and Dance Supply Store.** Start a venture which designs and manufactures portable theatre footlights, smoke for dance floors, lighting, special effects, sound systems, etc. Potential buyers include: amateur theatre and dance groups, rock groups, children's entertainers, variety entertainers, nightclubs and mobile disk jockeys.

107. **Rent computers to private business users.** The computers you rent might be new and/or second hand. Also rent out peripherals such as printers, stands and sheet feeders. Use local media to inform potential customers about your service. Postcards would work well here. Cost of computers has come down dramatically over the years but still a sizeable market for this business.

108. **Buy original computer game programs from home computer enthusiasts.** Find these programs by advertising in computing magazines. Produce a compilation of the programs on a master thumb drive. Watch copyrights, but sell on EBay or Craigslist.

109. **College and Test Prep.** Produce a series of low cost audio CD's or MP3's which help school students prepare for college for their PSAT, ACT and SAT tests for public examinations.

Also, just a general how to take examinations successfully audio too. You might give these CD's or MP3's a brand name like 'Personal School Revision CD's or MP3's". Get them stocked at Amazon, bookshops and specialty websites.

110. **Travel Planner.** While anyone can check an aggregator site for the best price to fly to Saint Louis, but planning a more elaborate trip might be too much for some travellers. This is where a travel planner comes in, using his skills to find the best trip—including flight, accommodation, rental car, and tours—for the budget. Visit **http://builditstrong.worldventures.biz/** too for best rates guaranteed for hotels, airfare and car rentals. Pretty cool.

111. **Computer Techs Getaways.** Organize educational (and fun) holidays and weekend breaks for computer enthusiasts who want to further their programming skills but also want to unwind from their stressful day-to-day routines. The courses might be held at a bed and breakfast house out of season in the mountains or at a beach house. Advertise in computing and travel magazines.

112. **Become a Blogger.** Many businesses hire bloggers to create attractive and relatable content for their websites. You don't have to limit your job search to local businesses, however, for this one, as the work is generally remote and submitted online. You can even be proactive and reach out to your favorite blogs to see if they are looking for contributors.

You can work for yourself as well and monetize your posts with affiliate offers that readers can purchase. You'll receive a percentage of the sale. Also, with the work being remote and not having to travel to one location each day, you can offer your services to multiple businesses too. This means multiple opportunities and more checks for your work. Social media today, is king. Learn to navigate it and create buzz and you will have a bright future here.

113. **Use luminous paint** of the kind used on watches and alarm clocks to highlight figures on natural ornaments such as starfish, coral, colorful rocks, pine cones, etc. Place these in a sheltered display case to illustrate their luminosity. Have display cases on show at gift shops.

114. **Homemade Custom Paper.** Start an enterprise which makes a high quality, home-made paper. Sell the paper at a premium for use as: Personal stationery, certificate presentation scrolls, printing paper for manually operated printing presses, etc.

115. **Lucky Charms & Good Luck Items**. People are superstitious. Bring out a selection of lucky charms which are for hanging from windscreens of cars, vans and trucks.

Buyers might want mini horse shoes, rabbit's feet, wooden or plastic number sevens, four-leaf clovers, etc. Package your lucky charms to distribute to a wide range of retailers especially around "Powerball, Super-Lotto and Mega Million" lotteries when prize money is the highest. We need all the luck we can get...right?

**116. Manufacture kits for making mosaics.** Each kit will have a pre-designed mosaic and people will have to complete it like a jigsaw puzzle. Use ads in craft magazines to sell kits by mail order.

**117. Greenhouses**. Sell greenhouse kits and finished greenhouses door-to-door. Buy the greenhouses from manufacturers at wholesale trade prices. Produce sales literature and recruit sales people to sell the greenhouses for you. Triage. Take the difference and reinvest.

**118. War Re-enactment.** Start a postal business which rents out war gaming model soldiers and other accessories. War gaming enthusiasts can use this service to play war games of any size from any period of history.

**119. Rent-a-Room.** If you have a spare room, take in a lodger or start a small-scale bed and breakfast business. If you choose the latter, either place a sign outside your house which reads 'Bed and Breakfast' or advertise in the windows of newsagents and in the classified ad columns of newspapers.

120. **Anatomical Charts.** Earn money from anatomical charts. Use the charts to: 1) Make stylish framed prints. 2) Make unusual designs for T-shirts. 3) Decorate household products such as wastepaper bins and lampshades. 4) Make decorative or educational posters. or, 5) Make a collection of educational slides. Sell these to doctors and medical professionals.

121. **Wine bottle art.** Make decorations for wine bottles. Each decoration is slipped over the neck of a bottle. These decorations are either wood carved or metal engraved with the name of a restaurant or family. Or, make floral decorations, the scent of the flowers complimenting the bouquet of the wine.

122. **Unusual Table Lamps**. Start a crafts business which makes unusual table lamps. Each lamp might feature a stand made of a conch shell, for example, or a Victorian bottle. If you hit upon a design which is popular, make sure that there are no problems for obtaining raw materials, as this could hinder you from making this a full-time business.

123. **Make Jewelry**. Take up the craft of Jewelry making and as soon as you acquire a basic skill, start selling what you make. Begin by sending for a catalog issued by a mail or online Jewelry making supplier. See what they are doing, how they've photographed the jewelry pieces and described the piece in its description. Sell first to your social media friends list, and then spread out and sell on Craigslist and Etsy.

124. **Weaving and Spinning Equipment Supply**. Start a mail or online store which sells equipment and supplies to weavers and spinners. An important market will be those taking up weaving and spinning for the first time. Place ads in crafts magazines which are directed at this group.

125. **Children's Height Chart Design**. Produce souvenir children's height charts which feature postcard-type views of local scenery. Or do souvenir suntan charts. These suntan charts have a complete range of skin shades. A holiday-maker buys a suntan chart to make a before and after comparison.

126. **Meal Planner.** One of the best ways to keep a grocery budget—and a waistline—in check, is to do meal planning. But for some, this kind of planning is a mystery wrapped up in a question mark. A meal planner could put together a list of a week's recipes, along with a grocery list, for a harried but budget-conscious family.

127. **Housing Remodeling**. Organize courses about how to build your own house extension, bathroom and kitchen remodels or family room redesign. Hold the courses during the weekends at the construction site of an extension or conversion. Or a bed and breakfast house could be hired out of season for a week-long course.

128. **Look Up In The Sky!** If you have a drone with photographic ability, you can call private homeowners, large estates, and businesses where there is certainly money to be made, in taking aerial drone photos of these homes and businesses. Show potential customers samples of your work. Also offer a framing service as well.

129. **Child Proofing Business.** Congratulations you baby is running around the house now. Amazing isn't it? But now they are also getting into everything under the kitchen sink. Keeping our kids safe is so important, but the details of how to do so can be confusing. A professional child proofing business is inexpensive to start up, but there may be state regulations to follow. It's also a good idea to apprentice with a child proofer in order to learn the business.

130. **Start a school for writers**. Provide tuition for people who want to either, improve their writing skills or earn money from writing their books and publishing them on the major book platforms.

Give instruction during the evenings and weekends. Also develop a "how to course" on how to put together your book and publish it in 7 days. Prospective writers will love it.

131. **Become a calligrapher of poems**. Earn money from calligraphy poems to commission for poets and sweethearts. a) Classic poems like 'Desiderata', 'Charge of the Light Brigade', etc., and selling them as gift products. b) Poems of local origin and selling them as souvenirs. Add children's books to your repertoire.

132. **Home Paintings**. If you have the artistic ability to sketch or do ink drawings of private houses there is certainly money to be made here. Get work by calling on households in the nicer looking parts of town and showing potential customers samples of your work. Also offer a framing service.

133. **Become a Mobile DJ**. Mobile disk jockey and emcee services can bring real like to an event. Having the sound equipment and music is the first step. Contact every event coordinator in your market and share your business card and brochure with them. Generally events are for several hours. DJs also become great emcees as they interview attendees and vendors and create real awareness of the value of the event in the process. You will be the most remembered person at any event if you've done a great job.

134. **Portrait Artists**. Become a portrait artist and work from of a shopping kiosk or booth, or a craft fair or flea market to start.

135. **Publish a 'Who's Who of Business Opportunities'.** Sell advertising space in this publication to business opportunity firms. Use direct mail and ads in the business opportunity press to sell advertising space and the finished publication.

136. **Open a small private school of art**. Employ artists to teach courses about different kinds of art from oil painting to pottery. Offer holiday courses, individual tuition and evening and weekend classes. Be willing to teach at the local Junior College as well during summers. Many students will want to take private instructions and register for your art school.

137. **Have an extra room in your home?** Rent it out to college students, missionaries or others that you've qualified. In large cities and towns, that can be $500-$1200 a month for a bedroom, access to a bathroom and kitchen privileges. What can you do with an extra $6,000 to $14,400 a year?

138. **Artistic Directory.** Create a directory for all artists, such as painters, illustrators, pottery workers and sculptors. Provide work for the artists and specialize in contacting businesses which might not have considered using artists.

For example, arrange for murals to be painted in staff canteens and sports clubs.

139. **Become a house painter**. Paint outside houses and businesses with a paint sprayer and roll and brush indoor rooms. Apply trims and cleanup. Big money in painting. Becoming a contractor is fairly easy, as customers will generally ask. You'll also be able to get more your time also.

140. **Become a Contractors School.** Help aspiring contractors become licensed contractors by preparing them in their field to take and pass the state's contractor's exam. This will help prepare general building contractors, painting contractors, plumbers, carpenters, wall board contractors, etc. to be prepared and pass those exams. Charge a flat fee for their preparation at various levels. Novice, experienced and test prep only.

141. **Care for the Disabled**. There is a real need in our society these days for those who care for the disabled, autistic, high and low functioning adults. The state in which you live has certain guidelines and requirements that you must meet in order to help and house these adults.

The state will pay you handsomely for your care. This is a long-term, 24/7/365 experience. If you have the patience and ability to care for others, this could be very rewarding work for you. In many cases, higher functioning adults attend a 9am-3pm daycare nearby where they can learn and earn money as well for some of their additional travel or expenses. It gives adult care providers a little breather each day too.

142. **Herbal Drink Supply**. Set up a mail or online business which sells equipment and supplies for making herbal drinks at home. This could be an interesting and healthy hobby for anyone to take up. Produce a small catalog online and advertise in a wide range of publications.

143. **Digital Media Conversion.** It's time consuming to convert old school media like CDs into digital files or old Super 8 and VHS movies and family photos and videos from vacations into a digital format.  If you have excellent tech skills, this is a service you can offer to the tech-phobic and time-crunched alike.

144. **Electronic Kits & Components**. If you are familiar with electronics, start a mail or online business which sells electronic kits, components and accessories. If possible bring out your own electronic kits. To obtain other products, email suppliers all over the world for what you need. Open your website with your catalog of available kits and electronic items your market is clamoring for.

145. **Patient Advocacy.** With the population of the world aging rapidly, and the complexity of our modern medical billing practices, there is a definite need for patient advocates. These individuals take the time to track down hospital billing paperwork and potentially argue with insurance companies. Considering the fact that many of those who need to hire advocates are either ailing or grieving, this is a very necessary service. Advocates can be paid by the hour or a percentage of what they believe they can save the patient.

146. **Open a school for disk jockeys.** Offer potential students different courses for radio, night-clubs, mobile discos, hospital radio and podcast radio. Give students training: in classes, on a one-to-one basis, or correspondence courses and through audio CD's, MP3's or DVD's. Radio still reaches more Americans each week then any single advertising medium. Find your niche.

147. **Supply a fortune teller or numerologist for parties and weddings**. A visiting fortune teller makes a party or wedding reception more entertaining for guests. Advertise your services on Craigslist and other free classified sites to start.

148. **Become a photographer's agent.** Sell the work of amateur photographers for a commission.

As an agent, your knowledge of the best place to sell photographs at home and abroad could lead to some amateurs becoming published photographers.

149. **Begin a mail or online business which sells folk crafts**. Pick a national group such as the Scots, Welsh, Irish, and American Indian, African American and Hispanic folk crafts. Put together folk craft products which capture the essence of your chosen group. Have a catalog printed (or digitized) and advertise it around the world.

150. **Conduct Informational Social Security and Medicare Seminars.** Charge attendees a fee for information and a luncheon/dinner at a local restaurant. Bring in a Social Security and Medicare expert to share with attendees the latest in benefits and perfect age to begin to receive their maximum Social Security benefits. This simple service will save attendees potentially hundreds or even thousands of dollars. You can also have a financial planner, pay you, to also attend and answer additional questions about estate planning, annuities, insurance and individual retirement account and how to take distribution without tax penalties.

151. **Candy Toffee Manufacturing.** Make a toffee of your own design and add a stick to make a toffee lollipop. Get them stocked at newsstands and confectioners or sell from a stall at markets, fairs and exhibitions.

152. **Job Interview Preparation**. Set up a school of 'Self-Promotion'. Teach students at your school how to sell themselves and impress others. For example: The opposite sex, work colleagues, job interviewers, etc. Hold classes, give individual instruction or teach people through audio CD's or MP3's or an annual membership website.

153. **Origami.** Start a mail or online firm which sells plans, books and supplies to origami hobbyists. Advertise your catalog in crafts magazines and your own online website.

154. **Become a professional family affairs adviser.** Just as a careers adviser gives advice on career improvement and development, your service gives advice on improving the future of an entire family. The advice might be about finance, careers, education, vacation planning, relationships, etc. There may be a need for certain licensing involved where financial advice is being given.

155. **Design and make leather stamp wallets for stamp collectors**. These would be for keeping duplicates and stamps for sale. The wallets might vary in size from the pocket to the desktop. Sell through stamp shops and adverts in stamp magazines.

156. **Fundraising Business**. Start a mail or online business which sells fund-raising accessories.

For example: booklets about fund-raising ideas, bingo calling machines, candy, pizza, popcorn sales, scratch cards and many, many others. Produce a digital catalog about your goods and send it to clubs, societies, associations, schools and everyone on your contact list.

**157. Debt Collection Course.** Put together a debt collection training course for small businesses. Every small business is a potential client. A key selling point is that the cost of the course should be quickly recovered from the more efficient collection of debts.

**158. Horse Racing.** Write and publish a book about betting on horses and racing. In this book, include details of betting systems and suggestions about how to assess the likely performance of horses. Sell copies of your book to horse racing enthusiasts from newspaper ads, direct mail and from your website.

**159. Kicking the Bad Habits Course.** Produce a series of audio CD's or MP3's about how to stop or reduce vices and bad habits. The CD's or MP3's might have titles like: 'How to Stop Snoring', 'How to Cut Down on Drinking', 'How to Pack Up Gambling', 'How to Stop Smoking', etc. Sell the CD's or MP3's by mail or online and through a wide range of stores and websites.

160. **Amateur Magician**. Put together a correspondence course about how to become an amateur magician. The aim would be teach people who to do numerous basic tricks. It would be a foundation course for amateur magicians. Also sell the products that magician's tricks require.

161. **Home or Antique Appraiser.** We all love the moment in ANTIQUES ROADSHOW when the owner learns how much their heirloom is worth. Becoming an antiques appraiser will allow you to live that moment every day. This does require a background education in the subject and access to an excellent reference library. Becoming a real estate appraiser, looks at comparables of real estate sold in the past 3-6 months and in many states requires 2000 hours of internship with a qualified appraiser to be certified. Both appraiser positions are unique and can be quite lucrative.

162. **Micro-Jobs.** With the advent of www.**Fiverr**.com we saw a brand new way to assign and accept work: little jobs for small payouts. But it's no party trick. Apps like **http://www.gigwalk.com/** and of course sites like **https://www.mturk.com/** make it possible to cobble together a living with lots of little assignments each day. And by the way, Fiverr has grown up since its $5 a gig days, though many gigs are still $5.00 plus $1 processing. To get a job done correctly and completely often times requires multiple gigs or

$25- $200 depending on the need. Great for folks with needs like a logo or ebook cover too.

163. **Floral Delivery to Businesses**. Start an enterprise which delivers table flowers on a regular basis to: restaurants, hair salons, dental surgeries, offices, etc. Call on these places to sell your services.

164. **Internet Affiliate Marketing**. If you already have your own website or blog, you can earn money by becoming an affiliate. You can sell products directly and earn money that way, or you can sign up others as affiliates with your own products and give them a percentage of the sales they make from your program, book, course or item. It's a great way to others to help you and you to help sell other people's products. Check out **www.Clickbank.com** for more information.

165. **Start a craft business which makes a selection of cactus products.** These products, such as paper weights, book ends, desk sets, etc. have live cactuses growing out of them. They are easy to maintain and can get a nice return.

166. **Make concrete mini-models of farm animals**. Each model is painted to look like a real farm animal. These are for gardeners to put on lawns to evoke the atmosphere of the countryside. Get them stocked at as many garden centers as possible. Large cows, barnyard chickens and even dinosaurs, can bring a different look to a farm, ranch or neighborhood.

167. **Sell garden fountains** to up-market householders. Produce quality sales literature and advertise in select magazines. Pay professional builders to do the building and installation work.

168. **Model Cars, Planes and Boats**. Buy ordinary plastic model kits of aircraft and boats. Construct the kits and hand paint them in their original colors. Sell the finished models from a stall at fairs and markets.

169. **Sell Burl and Manzanita Furniture**. Burl wood and manzanita. For example, a kit for making a rural scene might include wooden pieces cut in the shape of: trees, animals, clouds, buildings, etc. Sell either by mail or online to craft workers or through shops which sell craft products.

170. **Bulbs and Seeds**. Start a seasonal business which sells bulbs door-to-door. This business is best operated by two people: one calls on houses and the other moves a handcart full of bulbs.

171. **Start a collectable plate of the month club**. Commission the making of attractive plates and slowly build up a list of club members. While working this opportunity, create a plate-location, matching business too. When a plate of a set is broken, where can you find another to match it? You of course for a nice fee.

172. **Corporate Director Exchange**. Set up a company director exchange service. Your service arranges for one or two directors in different companies to swap places at board meetings. Use telephone or direct mail to sell your service to businesses. Or give your company the benefit of other director's insights and views. You may find a tremendous business advocate or partner in the mix too.

173. **Magazine Importer**. Import specialist magazines from overseas English-speaking countries. For example: magazines relating to unusual hobbies or sport. Your task is to build up lists of subscribers in this country. Begin by writing to overseas publishers to ask if they will supply magazines in bulk at good discount. Also, sell via an affiliate commission, magazines from various publishers. If you learn the best way to sell subscriptions, this could be very profitable.

174. **Weed Removal Service**. Begin and build a weed removal and control round. Operate this like a window cleaning service. You might do this work yourself or employ students or retired people.

175. **Product Demonstrators.** Ever been to s warehouse club store or busy supermarket on a weekend and see product demonstrators passing out samples of various goods for you to try?

These demo folks get paid $13 to $18.00/hour and more for their work. It's a combination of sales by exposing shoppers to the benefits of the products you're showing, and just great conversations with those who are passing by in a store who will try your product. Must be able to stand for a few hours. Regular breaks and lunches are given also.

176. **Profitable Flower & Live Plant Business**. Write and publish a series of booklets or CD's or MP3's about how to make money from flowers and plants. The titles might include: 'Starting a Florists', 'Setting up a Nursery', and 'How to Open a Garden Center'. Advertise in gardening magazines. Also expose your business on Craigslist and other free classified sites.

177. **Plant Rentals and Care.** Live plants, exotic plants, and hanging baskets. Your clients will include: offices, banks, pubs, hair salons, restaurants, exhibitions, etc. Also provide your clients with a maintenance service.

178. **Flower Arranging.** Learn about flower arranging at evening classes then, earn money from teaching others in your own home. Give afternoon classes to pensioners and housewives. A major attraction of the classes is that they act as a social occasion.

179. **Set up a production line which turns out mini-gardens in bowls and pots.** Sell from your own flea market booth or craft fair, through a range of retail outlets and online.

180. **Design and make herb gardens for the house or garden.** Produce the herb gardens in a range of different containers such as bottles, tubs, trays, large pots or hanging pots. Sell through suitable retailers or by mail or online.

181. **Devise a selection of scents specially designed for love letters and greeting cards.** For example, the scent of roses for love letters and pine trees for Christmas cards. Set up a business which manufactures, packages and distributes the scents.

182. **Bring out a range of herbal or hop filled pillows.** Make pillows for different functions, for example: pillows which are an aid for people who have difficulty sleeping, siesta pillows for the garden nap, pillows for the living room and pillows which are especially designed for daydreaming.

183. **Begin a business which rents out large and expensive astronomical telescopes** to householders who want to develop their interest in astronomy. Publicize your service at the local astronomy society and use local advertising to attract clients.

184. **Become a Marketing Consultant**. Whether you are helping a business with traditional marketing materials or instructing them on the fine art of blogging and social media, this is a business that has almost unlimited potential for freelancers. Median salary: $108,000 in the US for full-timers.

185. **Make wooden puzzles for children.** For example, brightly painted wooden shapes have to be fitted into the corresponding hole in a block of wood. Or make a flat wooden animal like a dinosaur or rabbit. Cut this animal into lots of wooden shapes so that it is a challenge to assemble.

186. **Hand-paint pictures or witty statements on plaques of wood**. For example, the pictures might feature animals and the statements might be about cooking like 'Oliver Twist's Favorite Kitchen'. Add a magnet to the back of each square so that they can be stuck to fridges and other metallic surfaces. Sell from your Etsy account.

187. **Seashell Business**. Set up a mail or online business which promotes the hobby of collecting seashells. Develop your online catalog which features your popular collection of seashells, beach items, and collector's accessories and books about seashells.

188. **Write and publish a newsletter about how to start a newsletter publishing business.** Each issue of the newsletter might be a lesson about one of the various topics involved in beginning and running a successful newsletter.

189. **Website Design.** Helping clients design the best website for their needs is a great way to make a living from home. It has become so much easier now with ready-made templates for WP (Word Press) and sites today are much more user friendly for visitors as well.  Google.com lists the median salary as of 2018, is $64,970. With websites today are easier than ever to construct, literally target every business on Main street in your community and triage (be the go between) those owners with those who know how to put sites together. Most business owners are overwhelmed in their startups and day-to-day operations to know what to do with their website. Good looking and functional websites can generate $1000-$3000 each depending the needs and complexity of the site. Learn all that you can about helping local business owners with their websites. Join the local Chamber of Commerce in your community too ($200 or less for a one-person operation) and you'll have a ready-made audience of needy website clients.

190. **Self-Improvement.** Start a mail or online business which sells health improvement books, booklets and audio CD's or MP3's.

Discover what titles are available from publishers and produce your own catalog. Affiliate programs work great here too, where you take a percentage (50-80%) of an author's price to sell their products as well. Also publish some of your own booklets and CD's or MP3's. Sell them from Amazon or EBay.

191. **The "BIG" Idea Factory**. Earn money by selling all sorts of ideas and information via website. For example: Topic ideas can be for DIY enthusiasts, housewives, hobbyists, craft workers, local businesses and many others. Produce either a general directory which has universal appeal or bring out specialized booklets for different markets. Ideas are the currency of business. Create new and exciting ideas in various market segments and watch others run with it and turn it into something special. Be the catalyst for change and progress.

192. **Stop Smoking.** Smoking kills 7 million people annually and it's rising throughout the world. Write a book and produce an audio CD/MP3 course for those who want to stop smoking once and for all. Smoking is a great scourge on society. Sell this through ads in newspapers, magazines or by Craigslist, other free classified sites and Amazon that have billions of eyeballs seeking out this information. Be relentless and save lives too.

193. **Self-Help and Self Improvement.** Create a series of booklets or CD's or MP3's which have titles like: 'How to Cure Boredom', 'How to Beat Depression', 'How to Get Out of a Rut', 'How to Beat Back Pain', etc. Sell via your website, through bookshops or other retail outlets.

194. **Instant Band Equipment**. Start a business that rents out drum kits, organs and electric guitars to those wanting to start their own Garage Band. Advertise your business both in the local press, high school newspapers and on Craigslist. Provide delivery to them. Get the monthly rental and deposit up front. We're talking kids here, who need to make monthly payments and be responsible for your equipment. If their band turn out to be a unique group, with real talent, represent them, and get them gigs in the community.

195. **Happiness Plants.** Make money from bringing out your own happiness plants. A happiness plant is any plant for which it can be claimed gives off an unseen fragrance which humans find pleasing. Sell from a market booth or online to local business people and homeowners.

196. **Talent and Beauty Institute**. This institute would be the beauty world's equivalent to 1) a finishing school (for women who want to become expert in doing their own make up) and 2) a secretarial school, (for women who want a career

in the beauty industry.) or 3) Women who would like a career in modelling or acting and want to know how to break in to that field.

197. **Street Advertising**. Start a walking menu board service (A sandwich board with a giant menu on it). Sell to restaurants and cafes throughout the region. Employ students and young people to carry the boards. Other ways to use street advertising is for local businesses to pay you $11-$15.00 an hour to twirl their sign about their product or service on your town's busiest intersections so the most people can see your sign. For example, a "Buy One Get One Free Sub Sandwich" with a huge red arrow pointing to the location or a big phone # on the sign where people can call in a lunch order.

198. **Special Event Photography**. At a busy tourist attraction, take portrait photographs of tourists as a family. Add a novelty to the photographs by, for example, dressing the tourists up in special costumes or having them stand behind cut-out of characters. Another example would be to dress clients in princess dresses or Wild-West outfits and add an aged appearance to the photos. Have additional clothing there for your clients that they can change into.

199. **Historical Photography.** Reprint old photographs of a town and mount them in attractive frames.

Sell them through local stores. Advertise in local press for residents who have old photographs you could pay a fee to have reproduced. Great for store owners to use to decorate their businesses and offices, but also for souvenirs for their customers as well.

200. **Sell Lucky Charms.** People are superstitious by nature and love items that will help them to be lucky at whatever they do. Create a business and an income by selling lucky charms at car-boat shows or through Shopify store or website. Sell, for example: Rabbits feet, horseshoes and four-leaf clovers. Start by tracking down trade sources of these lucky charms.

201. **Journaling and Diaries.** Start a blog/ vlog for journal and diary keepers. Most of us work in isolation and many journalers would welcome a blog /vlog post to inform them about the existence and activities of their fellow journalers. You YouTube channel, website or FaceBook Group page may act as a forum for discussion about diary writing and also give advice about how to improve upon the techniques of diary writing. Perhaps also create the perfect diary for your tribe, and sell it from Amazon. It's great when your followers are truly on the same page.

202. **Bible, Scripture and Hymn Pillows**. Buy old bibles and hymn books from churches and education authorities.

Have the pages shredded and use as stuffing material for 'bible' or 'hymn' pillows, teddy bear and other soft products. Also do 'bible' confetti and stuff bottles to make bottled bibles.

**203. Self-Improvement Writing Course**. Produce and sell a home study course on how to write self-improvement books. Writing this type of book is one of the easiest ways to become a published author. In this field there are always themes which sell well, such as how to make money, attract love, losing weight, dating tips and hacks, and how to be a real success.

**204. Music Blast from the Past.** We all remember our favorite music from the past right? Start an online business which specializes in selling classic singles and albums from the past. Classics are constantly being re-issued in various countries around the world. Import these and sell online at a premium.

**205. Coin Collecting Club**. Serve coin collectors by starting a coin of the month club. Activities might include sending collectors new foreign coins as they are issued. Creating a FaceBook Coin Collectors group helps to allow members to better communicate and share ideas with others. Membership to the FB Group is predicated on paid membership in the club.

**206. Drink Specialist.** Devise unique cocktail drinks and punches to commission. Name each drink after the person nominated by the sponsor.

These recipes make unusual gifts, for example, a specially designed punch would add fun to a wedding reception or birthday. Sell from classified ads and on Craigslist.

207. **Office Décor and Games**. Use direct mail or an online website to sell a range of novelties, games, toys, quizzes and ornaments and holiday décor for the office. Produce a catalog and send to offices.

208. **Rocketry & Drone Site**. Start an online business which sells books, equipment and supplies to those interested in amateur rocketry and drones. Put together an amateur rocketry kit for beginners and advertise this to attract new hobbyists to the business. Drones have become a very hot market so find a 100 ways to use a drone and then write your book for Amazon.

209. **Ornament Club**. Launch a carved ornament of the month club. A collection of beautifully carved ornaments will add character to a house and make a good investment. Imagine having 100 paying clients a month or more? Craigslist and other free sites is a great place to start here.

210. **Poetry On-Demand**. Compose poems to order for any occasion, such as engagements, births, weddings, birthdays, valentines, etc. These poems make a unique and memorable gift.

Use classified ads to sell your service. Or set up a booth at a fair or tourist site and compose poems on the spot. A website can give visitors an idea of what their selections are. Have a PayPal account attached for check out too.

211. **Radio Writing Course**. Radio is still the most listened to media in the US by far. Not TV or newspapers. Compile a correspondence course about writing drama, comedy or advertising for radio. Radio is a proven route to becoming a successful ad writer, drama or comedy writer. Your course would help people to develop their writing ability and help them into the path of this business.

212. **Left-Handers Shop.** Organize a range of products that are specially designed for left-handed people. 10% of the US market are left-handed. That's almost 35 million people! Have a catalog created for your online business.

213. **Japanese and Chinese Gardens**. Set up a garden improvement business which designs and builds ornamental Japanese or Chinese gardens. Produce a brochure about your work and advertise in up-market and gardening publications. Place brochures on doorsteps too in these up-markets. Advertise for free on Craigslist and other free classified sites, also.

214. **Metal, Gemstone and Ornament Art**. Use ball bearings to make attractive ornaments, either 1) decorate large ball bearings or 2) stick smaller ball bearings together. The ornaments might be shaped to look like people or animals. Sell through gift shops or from a craft fair booth. Also create little miners and glue them to cut agates or other crystals, pyrite or gemstones for a value added upsell. And they're beautiful conversation pieces in an executive office too.

215. **Be the Local Ticket Master**. Act as a sales agent for fan clubs, concert tickets etc. Sell hard to get tickets for a commission to popular concerts and festivals. Sell to people in your region. Find sources of popular tickets. Get PSA (public service announcements) from local radio stations who want to help their listeners attend the latest concerts. Get the source of tickets first and you'll be busy trying to keep up. We love our entertainment.

216. **Become an Entertainment Promoter.** This can be a huge business if you brand it properly and prepare every concert detail. Rock groups and musical performers, orchestras and comedy acts all have one thing in common...they have to work. You as a promoter will do just that...keep them working. Get with Colleges and High Schools about the rental of their gymnasiums and football fields for specific dates that artists are travelling through on tour.

Book that date and venue after you've contacted the artist to see what their costs to perform are. Factor that into your ticket sales and the amount of tickets you need to sell and advertising to promote the event and your profit at the end. Offer backstage VIP Passes for triple the ticket price. This VIP experience with the artist is perhaps the one thing that concert-goer has looked forward to their entire life. Give it to them. See this. **https://bit.ly/2F7ZXdT** . Run the numbers and see how you make $10k to $100k for these events. A whole checklist of things will need to be done too prior to the event like security, licensing, portable restrooms, back table t-shirt and memorabilia sales, CD and poster sales of the artist, and cleanup after the event. Plan for this and your life with the rich and famous may change.

217. **Paint Windows for Businesses**. Christmas isn't the only time to paint windows you know? Why not approach every single business in your area, with what you can do for them to systematically increase their sales. Offer them a spring, summer, fall and Christmas package. Depending on the number of window panes they have and the difficulty of the artwork, you can net 80-90% of the cost of the project per local business.

Brand yourself and open this up. Painting skills help, but after a few windows you'll know what your business owners want. Deliver flyers of your work (or what you can do for them) and base prices, to every business, large or small. As you begin to look at every business as a $1000 bill you'll see this opportunity differently. Now go have fun.

218. **Mounted Etchings**. Sell mounted etchings by calling on private households and shopkeepers. Buy from the original artist or from a wholesaler and mount and frame for sale.

219. **Telephone Sales Course**. The single most powerful tool in business is...the telephone! Produce an audio CD/MP3/DVD course about how to use the telephone to grow, maximize and double your sales, this year, for your business. Everyone in your business needs to know how to use the phone. Cover subjects such as telephone greetings for incoming and outgoing messages, selling and upselling on the phone, dealing with inquiries and complaints, interviewing, etc. Sell by phone or from your website. Advertise anywhere and everywhere you can. Start with Craigslist and a myriad of other free classified sites. Target business groups and forums on FaceBook too.

220. **Pen Pal Group on FaceBook**. Run a pen pal club. Produce daily blog posts to your lists of people looking for pen pals.

Also boost your income by selling advertising space ion your own site as well. Use small ads world-wide to recruit subscribers. Use Facebook too to get thousands of new subscribers.

221. **Interior Decorating Business**. Start an interior decoration business which specializes in period decor. For example decor with a theme related to the Victorian or Georgian age, the 1910s, 1920s or Art Nouveau. Produce a glossy brochure about your service and use ads in up-market publications to attract enquiries.

222. **Set up a direct mail marketing library**. It's like having a super marketing director on staff. For a fee, any business can borrow examples of previous direct mail campaigns. A client business might borrow the work of either competitors or potential clients with real world examples and results. A single new marketing campaign or way of thinking can double a company's sales and profits. Find out what is working for other businesses like yours and duplicate it and then go about to tweak it, and make it better. You may think that your clients come to you for a certain problem to be solved and they do...but they never find you with marketing. Every business owner must understand right up front, that they are in the marketing business fulltime.

223. **Hobby Library**. Create a library of audio CD's/MP3'sand DVDs about hobby subjects such as model making, angling, stamp collecting, coin collecting, treasure hunting, etc. These CD's or MP3's and DVDs might be about specialized areas within each hobby. Sell them from ads in hobby magazines or get them stocked at hobby shops. Also list these hobby items on your websites blog so that you can monetize it.

224. **Astrology Music**. Produce a separate audio CD/MP3 for each astrological star sign. Each CD/MP3 should feature music that matches up with the astrological sign's overview. Put the CDs and DVDs in a display box and sell them at music stores, online and at flea markets. Sell them also from your website too.

225. **Tug-of-War Rope**. Market a tug-of-war rope. Package the rope and get it stocked at sports or toy shops respectively. A short rope for adults and a toy rope for children could be used to play small scale games of tug of war. Or the rope could be attached to a wall to make an exercise device.

226. **Office Equipment Rental Business**. Rent out photocopying machines on a temporary basis. These machine might be rented by the day, week, month or the year.

Businesses many times have a need for large copy runs and even though copy printing is much cheaper online today there is still a need. Also provide the printing/ copy service yourself. Need additional computing and the company can absorb a monthly rental expense, but now an outright purchase? Then Rent.

227. **Super Hero Booth.** Open a flea market booth which sells celebrity and super hero products and photos with the super hero. Sell books, badges, posters and other products on the latest celebrities and super heroes. These celebrities will include new pop stars, film stars, models and national heroes. Also sell products about classic celebrities like the Beatles, Rolling Stones and Elvis.

228. **Organize pop or rock music talent contests.** The income from each contest would come from either, charging the performers an entrance fee or selling tickets to the public. You may even be able to find a sponsor to back the entire contest and get radio and local TV stations to promote it.

229. **Design and produce a range of children's badges.** These might feature pictures of animals, spacecraft, robots or funny faces. Mount them on a felt covered board or place them in small cellophane packets. Have them displayed at newsstands and toy shops.

230. **Bubble Mix.** Sell home-made bubble mixture to children at markets, roadside sites, fairgrounds and fetes. Give each child a ring made from soft wire to make the bubbles with.

231. **Halloween Costumes.** Make military play uniforms for boys and princess and cute costumes for girls. For example: 7th Cavalry, navy uniforms, toy soldier uniforms, 101$^{st}$ Airborne, etc. From animal costumes, to bumblebees and zebra costumes why not make Halloween a fun time of the year. Package and sell through online toy stores and of course, your own website. Alternatively have an online catalog produced. Very strong sales for Halloween from mid-August to October 31$^{st}$. Spirit Costumes has a year-round ongoing business. Here's their fan page on FaceBook. Check it out. **https://www.facebook.com/spirithalloween/** for ideas.

232. **Political Campaign Manager**. Do you like politics? Some people love it and are very good at telling the political story of the issues and the people surrounding them. Why not look to become a Campaign Manager for a local candidate or initiative? Take your knowledge of fund-raising, marketing, social media and sharing your candidate's view on the issues, and turn that into a political consultant and begin earning money for from it by helping local candidates first and then moving up with each successful campaign.

Campaign Managers and Finance Managers are paid well in large campaigns. Expect to make 10-15% minimum of funds raised in a local election. A salary for a larger campaign.

233. **Psychological Help Information.** Produce a library of audio CD's or MP3's which give advice about health and psychological problems experienced by men and women. Draw up lists which are unique to men and to women. Some licensing and credentials may be required. Check your state for those requirements. Sell by mail and online through your website. Consider promoting it through free websites like Craigslist and even EBay for a small fee.

234. **Start a vegetarian food catering service.** Devise a menu with imaginative meals. Advertise in healthy, political and environmental publications. Charge $7-8/meal for 90 meals in a month. Get paid in advance and deliver the most amazing food to your clients they've ever eaten! Word of mouth is all you'll probably need. Deliver meals every week.

235. **Cosmetic Sales Booth.** Have a flea market booth that sells cosmetics. Cosmetics usually have good profit margins and a flea market booth has low overhead and provides a place for your return clients to come back to. These two factors combined make it an attractive business opportunity. Women will find it hard to resist a great value in cosmetics. Trust me.

236. **Cinema & Film School**. Start a school for the cinema and film students. Compile a variety of courses about different genres of the cinema such as westerns, science fiction and musicals. Teach them how to write, capture, direct and produce short-films to start and feature films later as they progress through your program. This is a tuition based program so you will need to cover all your expenses and make a profit with what you charge your students. Film schools typically charge $70k to $100k to attend. Offer a certification or film school degree to get public funding for your students, Not Produce a prospectus and advertise in cinema and film magazines.

237. **Local Handy Man Service.** Establish a dial-a-handyman service. Produce a flyer which lists examples of the jobs you do and your prices. Deliver flyers and unique business cards to households and businesses in your area. Use voice mail to take calls while you're out. Get a free phone number that can be used solely for your business at **https://voice.google.com**. Advertise in Craigslist and other free online classified ad sites to start.

238. **Delivery Business**. Start a delivery business with your van, which works for importers and small manufacturers. Build up a complimentary range of products from different importers and manufacturers and call on potential customers.

Examples of product ranges are health foods, hobby supplies, sportswear and electrical goods. Be the best, most reliable delivery person you can be and jobs will come your way easily.

239. **Kiosk Sales**. Especially during the summer and "sunny months" selling sunglasses anywhere you can throw up a table is big business. Many entrepreneurs have rented mall kiosks to sell sunglasses and accessories and do exceptionally well. Why? We all lose our sunglasses or need them for our trip home. There a dozens of name brand knock-off companies that are willing and able to help you. Sales will taper off slightly in colder months, but sunglasses are sold every day of the year. Margins are always high too. Check out these suppliers here. **https://bit.ly/2qOV7hy.** You'll see what I mean. At the end of that season, prepare for Halloween and Christmas by selling gifts, costumes, and teddy bears, for example. Wherever you can custom make costumes, teddy bears by dressing them up, you've got a winning combination for a year round kiosk.

240. **Capture The Moment Souvenirs.** Begin a business which bottles sea or lake water from famous places. Sell the bottles as either souvenirs, i.e. 'pocket or desktop Atlantic Ocean' or a natural beauty treatment, i.e. 'bathe your face in natural lake water' packaged in larger 64oz bottles.

241. **Business Research Center**. Research, write and publish a series of booklets about how to start and run specific home businesses. Examples of titles might include: 'Money from Typing at Home', 'Your Own Telephone Sales Business', 'Your Own Knitting Business', etc. Sell by mail order.

242. **Paperweight Business**. Make novel paperweights by modifying: tennis balls, golf balls, baseballs, pool balls, etc. Get them stocked at stationers, sports clubs and gift shops. Expand and do other paperweight items like unique geode rocks or crystal coasters to affect your drinking bottle water, etc. Get creative here.

243. **Luggage Tags.** Make a selection of soft toy or fabric luggage tags for travelers. For example, a normal luggage tag is accompanied by two small dice made from soft toy materials. Alternatively make a range of soft toy luggage tags which are designed to act as travel mascots. Fun too. Sell online.

244. **Organic Fruit and Vegetable Sales**. Package individual apples, oranges and bananas. Sell through newsstands and other suitable local stores. Make them organic and raise the prices.

245. **Mystery and Crime Series.** Produce a series of audio CD's or MP3's about the crimes of the century.

The crimes covered might include: mass murders, bank robberies, arson and fraud. Sell these CD's or MP3's by direct mail, mail or online or get them stocked at bookshops and newsstands. Sell through your own website too and promote it.

**246. Design a log book for the house.** This is to record every physical change to a house so a householder can: Analyze costs, plan future changes and have the feeling of being well organized. Arrange for the log book to be printed and sell to householders direct or through Amazon.

**247. Design a sport log book so that sport enthusiasts** can keep a record of their performance. Get copies printed and sell to shops or sell from ads in sports magazines.

**248. Insect Study Material**. Make a selection of soft toy insects. For example: caterpillars, ladybirds, bumblebees and wasps. Package the soft toys and claim that everyone should have a pet insect. Another crazy idea might be to create your own ant farms and sell them. Develop plastic cages for all sorts of insects. You can watch them and see how insects react with other bugs too.

**249. Develop a range of cake decorations with dozens of themes.** Use these and promote them for birthday parties, sports team games, weddings and receptions and business gatherings. Learn your craft by taking cake decorating classes and learning new techniques from DVD's on the subject. Promote yourself and your business through social media, wedding publications, Craigslist, etc.

**250. Make rosettes.** Add to each rosette either a calligraphic or printed label which reads 'Cook of the Year', 'Prize Winning Mother', or 'Dad of the Year'. Have them displayed in local shops.

**251. Make soft toy lucky charms**. One idea is a giant number seven. Other ideas include: four leaf clovers, horseshoes, rabbits feet and destiny dice.

**252. Mobile Mechanic.** Start a mobile installation and repair service for all kinds of car problems. Put together a flyer which lists prices for different jobs. Car owners will save these in their glove boxes in case they have a problem. Deliver your flyers to houses or stick them behind windshield wipers of cars in your area.

**253. Antique Appraising**. Set up a service which gives independent valuations and assessments for those considering the purchase of a particular expensive antique.

**254. Use clothes pegs to make souvenir ornaments**. These might take the form of animals, castles or boats, windmills and many others. Also design and produce kits so that craft workers can make their own ornaments from clothes pegs. Sell by mail order.

**255. Holiday Gift Exchanges**. Arrange holiday exchanges between various English speaking nationalities such as English, Scottish, Americans, Australians and Canadians. You might either provide a personal service which matches people or publish an online listing for people seeking gift exchanges.

**256. Local History Book**. Every large city and even small towns need their own history told. Create a book which has a title like "101 Unusual Facts about Our Town." Discover these facts by reading local history books and visiting the archives of local newspapers and visiting your local historical society. You could do similar booklets about a variety of towns and specialize in those which are popular with tourists. Publish your books through **www.lulu.com** and purchase a few hundred copies at wholesale. Sell the books to local established businesses, the library and historical societies so that they can resell them at the cover price.

**257. Rack Display Business.** Bring out an information package about 'How to Start Your Own Carded Products Business' (ordinary products are mounted on card for displaying on racks or walls in shops). From sunglasses and reading glasses to refrigerator magnets, to recently viewed DVD's and motivational CDs. An information package might consist of CD's or DVDs on sales dialogue, booklets and diagrams about your ideas and billing per rack of products. Approach individual businesses to test their interest.

258. **Badge Designer**. Design and produce your own badges. These might have designs which feature sports, witty statements, pop stars or flowers, etc. Mount on specially printed display cards and sell cards to shops.

259. **Low Entry Antique Sales.** Start a flea market booth which sells beautiful but low valued antiques. Obtain stock from either trade sources or buy saleable goods from the public or import from places like **www.alibaba.com**

260. **Badge Sales.** Earn money from selling badges at pop concerts, festivals, tourist sites and other places where there are crowds.

261. **Geology Specimen Sales**. Put together an online service which sells rocks and mineral specimens to collectors. Produce a catalog which lists a wide range of minerals and rock specimens. Also include in the catalog collector's supplies and accessories. Get notoriety for your rocks by displaying them at county fairs too.

262. **Aerial Photography.** Collect and take a wide range of aerial photographs. These might be high altitude shots of villages, towns or cities. Start an online business which frames and sells these photographs. Use PayPal as your payment platform.

263. **House Name Signs**. Slice timber logs and burn letters into the wood to make house name signs. Also varnish them and sell from a stall at special markets or get examples stocked at retailers who would take orders for you.

264. **Special Stationary Created**. Produce writing paper which has borders printed with pretty rural scenery or flowers. Get this stocked at stationers and tourist shops.

265. **Prepare Astrological Readings and Charts about Family Ancestors**. Use astrology readings and charts to shed light on personal characteristics of ancestors. Advertise in genealogy publications.

266. **Lawn Ornaments**. Organize the production of concrete or plastic garden gnomes and statues. Have them stocked at garden centers and retailers who sell garden products.

267. **Poker & Texas Hold 'em**. Prepare a book and course about how to increase your chances of winning at poker, and primarily Texas Hold' em. The course allows people to develop their skills over a period of time and allows you to charge a reasonable amount of money. Teach systems on how to win consistently, learn bluffing and the odds on every hand based on the cards you hold. Use press advertising to sell it and open it up to Craigslist and other free classified sites.

268. **Nut Re-Packaging**. This may sound a little nutty, pun intended, but there are many people who are taking bulk nuts like pistachios, and raw and smoked almonds, purchasing them from local producers and repackaging them in 1-2 ounce food quality bags, with labels and selling them to C-Stores (convenience stores) for a very high markup. C-Stores can't get these nuts reasonably without many layers of distribution. Sell these direct on a monthly route to every C-Store you can and watch what happens. I knew someone who made an amazing income doing this. You can too.

269. **Special T-shirt Designs**. Design, produce and distribute T-shirts and sweatshirts which have an astronomical theme. The idea is that people will buy a T-shirt or sweat shirt that celebrates their star sign. Package them and have them displayed at a wide range of retailers.

270. **Horse Drawn Carriage Rides**. Set up a horse drawn carriage ride service in a tourist town or resort. Provide a short trip around places of interest. Rent out for special wedding entries too in parks. Target wedding planners and bridal stores where brides share what they want to see happen at their wedding.

271. **Open a school of creativity.** Teach business people about the various techniques of creative thinking, such as brainstorming, lateral thinking, quick think, value analysis, etc.

Hold classes or give personal training during work hours or lunch breaks. Can you develop ten new ideas every day? I bet you can if you try. Write tm down.

272. **Biographies.** Produce a series of famous biographical audio CD's or MP3's about famous artists, writers, politicians, inventors, film stars, etc. Sell these through bookshops and from your website.

273. **Sightseeing Tour Guides**. Start a novel tourist service in the center of a tourist town. Carry a tourist on a short tour of the city and sightseeing areas. In places like Sedona, Arizona, for example, one of the tour guide companies is the **https://www.pinkadventuretours.com/**. Get an idea of how to do this in other areas of the country and duplicate.

274. **Surfing Instructor**. Teach want-to-be surfers all that they need to do to be proficient at surfing the waves near your beach community. You could advertise on Craigslist or local publications. Offer surf board rentals, beach wear, sunglasses and surf board waxing too. Have a shop near the beach. Surf's up!

275. **Holiday Trip Organizer.** Organize outdoor holidays in America. For example, walking or cycling holidays in the Rockies. Sell places on these holidays to people in Britain and the rest of Europe.

276. **Unique Holiday Travel Ideas.** Write and publish a booklet about '101 Ideas for Off the Beaten Track Holidays'. Get this publication stocked at bookshops or sell from Amazon as an e-book. You might also sell advertising space to firms who organize unusual holidays.

277. **Christmas Decorator.** Hang and take down Christmas lights and decorations for homeowners and businesses who just don't want to do it any longer. Offer a Christmas tree setup plan too. Take orders and payments in advance. It gets crazy quick in November.

278. **Wedding Planner.** Set up a business which organizes weddings. Compile a list of tasks which need to be done to make a wedding successful. Put together a selection of packages at different prices and sell these to potential brides and families.

279. **Collectable Plates, Spoons & Thimbles**. Open a booth at an antiques fair, craft show or flea market. Sell collectable plates, spoons and thimbles as collectables. Buy your stock from manufacturers, wholesalers' importers and collectors.

280. **Role Playing Games.** Devise and produce biblical role playing games. For example, people might take the roles of characters in parables.

Arrange for the games to be manufactured. Sell by post or get them stocked at shops, particularly shops specializing in religion.

**281. Pen Pal Club for Literature of Math.** Start a pen pal club for children and adults who have an interest in literature or math. Members of the club can write to each other about books or blog posts they read. Advertise in literary publications, and Craigslist around the world.

**282. World War II Library**. There is a lot of material about WW2. Produce a library of audio CD's or MP3's and old video about the history of World War II. The advantage of these CD's or MP3's is that they can feature the sounds of historic events and tell a story that many have forgotten or never heard. Have them stocked at shops which sell books or records or create an online catalog and set up your business. Approach VFW them (Veterans of Foreign Wars) and offer the share stories with them from the material.

**283. Art from Foreign Coins.** Use low value foreign coins to make unusual pictures. For example, might be either a coin mosaic or a selection of coins mounted next to each other to make silhouettes of landscapes. Frame the pictures and get them stocked at shops which sell gifts, coins or souvenirs.

284. **Spanish Language Learning.** Put together an audio CD/MP3 course about teach yourself the Spanish language. Sell the course by mail order and get it stocked at bookshops and souvenir shops throughout the community. If there are already great courses out there, then find a way to sell them through an affiliate program and get 50-75% commission.

285. **Financial Planning Charts**. Produce wall-charts which helps individuals and couples manage their financial affairs better. A thorough record of expenditures is made on the wall-chart. The wall-chart helps to make it easy to control finances because it is so visible to all. Have a place and date on the chart for paying off items like (cars or credit cards). This can act as a real motivator to keep the family budget too. Attach plastic envelopes on the chart, if you wish, to put extra money towards a particular bill or vacation, for example.

286. **Bar & Drinking Games**. Create an online business which sells drinking accessories and memorabilia. For example, yard-long drinking glasses, personalized shot glasses. Traditional bar/pub games, darts, collectable beer mats, books on how to mix drinks, and a book about the various breweries and brands from around the world.

287. **Music Group Advance Team**. Start a service which produces the high quality, demonstration audio CD's or MP3's for a new pop group.

The groups will pay for the production of the CD's or MP3's. Your service also distributes copies to people in the music business. Advertise in the music press and hand-deliver to radio stations in the area. Mail them to others out of the area.

288. **Inventing Business.** Write, produce and sell a training course about inventing for profit. The course would help a person develop their creative abilities and then identify areas where small inventors would get the most patents. A key selling point of your course is that inventing is both fun and lucrative. Teach how to secure a patent. Learn about the four different kinds of patents and become the local expert.

289. **Traditionally Painted Postcards**. Produce a selection of postcards which feature traditional oil paintings and water color paintings of tourist sites. The paintings featured might be contemporary or historical. Sell to stores and gift shops around the tourist site.

290. **Reproduce Stone Monuments**. Organize the building of reproduction stone monuments. The reasons why anyone might want a reproduction monument might include: personal gratification, to create a tourist site, to attract customers to a business, etc.

291. **Recycling and Upcycling Specialist**. Always recycle your plastic bottles and your aluminum cans.

Lots of money is saved and the environment is improved when you take it seriously. Also visit Upcycle.com and then sell on free sale sites from stuff you've found in thrift stores. There's money in recycling folks.

292. **Start a Business Club**. Begin a lesson of the month club for those who want to start a business. Each lesson would be like a monthly newsletter and would be part of a comprehensive course. The lessons might be about starting a business either in general, or about a specific type of business such as creating a successful Shopify or Etsy store.

293. **Scientific Book of Experiments.** Create a company which designs and manufactures children's kits for, making kaleidoscopes, constructing pinhole cameras, growing crystals, and other things which demonstrate simple scientific principles. You might include all the projects in a book of basic scientific experiments.

294. **Children's Novelties and Jokes**. Put together a box of children's jokes and novelties. In each box include many of the products popular with children such as card tricks, itching powder, plastic spiders and cockroaches, etc. Get these small boxes stocked at toy shops. Sell at garage sales and flea markets too and of course online from your own website.

295. **Wooden Toys for Children**. Begin a woodwork business which makes toys for children which are variations of the traditional rocking horse, toy chest, etc. For example, rocking mythical creatures, rocking rafts with a single sail, airplanes, UFOs, etc. Sell finished toys or kits through toy shops or online.

296. **Mosaic Art.** Make small and attractive mosaics for hanging on walls like paintings. For example, a mosaic might be circular and feature the face of a goddess from the ancient world.

297. **Bridge and Chess Products**. Sell products related to the game of bridge and chess. Conduct a world-wide search for products related to bridge and. chess. Produce a catalog and advertise in up-market national publications and online at your website.

298. **Goalkeeper Clothing**. Design and make a selection of gloves for Football/Soccer goalkeepers. Try to add some special feature such as 'extra lightweight', 'extra tough', or 'extra warm'. Have them stocked at sports shops for children and adults.

299. **Pen Leather Protectors**. Use leather fabrics to make pen wallets and pencil cases. Sell the wallets and cases empty or buy pens and pencils at trade prices and fill the wallets and cases to make a finished product.

300. **Second Hand Bookstore**. Set up an online business which sells second-hand books. Use your own books for the initial stock. Find further stock by advertising for both trade source and complete collections from private individuals and buying at thrift stores and garage sales. Produce lists and place ads in various free publications and Craigslist for example.

301. **Enlarge Your Vocabulary.** Increasing your vocabulary gives you a real edge in the workplace. Give training to those who want to enlarge their vocabulary. Your advertising material might include a word test similar to Reader's Digest's 'Test Your Word Power' and an offer to improve the score.

302. **State and Federal Labor Law Posters**. Every American business should have these Federal and State regulation boards posted somewhere in their business. Generally the break rooms. Hours and overtime rules, company tardiness policies, minimum wage posting by year, along with Staff notices, fire instructions, health and safety rules, productivity figures, etc. Call on businesses to sell the boards and include a free installation service in your offer. See what I mean here. **https://bit.ly/2qQB5mS**. Buy for about $20.00 and sell installed for $55 or $60.00. The businesses will then be in compliance with the Labor Laws of the state and love you.

303. **Teach Crafting.** If you are an expert on crafts, earn money from teaching it in quiet corners or back rooms of shops which sell wools, crafts, artists and painting materials or picture framing services.

304. **Become a Locksmith**. If you are mechanical by nature, things like locks and safes may be up your alley. Learn your craft from a certified locksmithing school and learn to help drivers with their locked keys in their cars, safe picking for customers who have forgotten their combinations and of course, key making for cars, homes and businesses. Locksmith certification and training is between $700 for home study course and up to $3000 for on-hands training. Locksmiths like to say, "If you think it's expensive to hire a professional locksmith, try hiring an amateur." Locksmiths make good money too. The median annual Locksmith salary is $49,864, as of March 29, 2018, with a range usually between $43,257 and $56,215, however this can vary widely depending on a variety of factors.

305. **Golf Putting Instruction**. In golf, almost half of all shots are putts. With that being said, help business executives (and all golfers for that matter) improve their golf putting at the office by selling them a DVD, tips and hacks on how to reduce the number of putts they take in game of golf and  a book to reinforce the DVD instruction.

Sell in golf magazines, FaceBook Golf Groups and Forums, and from your own website. Target golfers all day log with a great offer. If you're a golf pro at a local club, you can use this an introduction to pro golf lessons.

**306. Lace Jewelry**. Use lace to make unusual Jewelry, such as lace bracelets, lace earrings, brooches and necklaces. Let your imagination run wild to create the design of each item of Jewelry. For example, embed lace in clear plastic.

**307. Learning to Ace Jeopardy**. When you know things, life is just easier. Learn all that can with a general knowledge of many topics put together in your online course complete with multiple choice tests. In your advertising emphasize that a better life might result from taking the course.

**308. Learn and then teach origami.** Also, if you have a flair for making animals in an interesting technique, earn money from doing origami as entertainment for groups.

**309. Lingerie Passion Parties.** A LINGERIE PARTY is a type of party plan for selling women's lingerie products. A social event is used to display products to guests, and then to take orders for the products before the gathering ends. These parties are usually held in lingerie stores, but they have become increasingly popular as home parties. Those that host a party get a hostess gift too.

310. **Start a fishing companion finding service.** Take details of when an angler is available, their interests, age and level of skill. Offer members of your service various suitable partners. Place ads in angling publications to attract customers. Also use Craigslist to get it started.

311. **One Man Show**. Put together a one-man theatrical show which is pleasant to watch. For example, recite highlights from Shakespeare or the work of a well-known poet or your own interesting biography. Perform your show on stages, at local clubs, coffee shops, or even offices during the lunch hour, parties and private households.

312. **Self-Improvement Letter.** Write and publish a newsletter which deals with the most important aspects of self-improvement. The newsletter might consist of ideas for getting ahead and mini courses about appearance, self.-image development, public speaking, overcoming stage fright, etc. Sell subscriptions internationally.

313. **Start a thimble of the month club** for new and established thimble collectors. Members of the club receive the club's choice of thimble of the month.

314. **Become a professional organizer of private and business parties**. You provide clients with a comprehensive service which does everything from supplying caterers, and

security to organizing a coat checking service. Advertise your service in a wide variety of publications.

**315. Local Folklore Book**. Produce a series of audio CD's or MP3's or books about the folklore of your region. Have them stocked at local shops and historical societies.

**316. Organize Cruise Trips for Business Executives and their Spouse.** Advertise a year in advance as executives need to plan their time off as well. Bring in high level speakers and seminar gurus to share their insights with those who attend. On a 4-day cruise for example, have two sessions for one hour each per day of instruction and personal development. The rest of the day is yours to enjoy. Combining relation and a business seminar everyday makes this a great write-off too. Another side benefit of organizing these trips, is that for every 15 tickets that you sell you get a ticket free.

**317. Organize board game playing holidays** and weekend breaks. Guests might play: the latest fashionable board games, etc.

**318. Personal Safety Parties.** With crime in many areas of the country on the rise, men and especially women can be vulnerable in parking lots, hallways, alleyways and even out in open areas. Enter the personal safety parties from various companies.

Here's one. **https://damselindefense.net**/ for example, sells pepper spray in many shapes and sizes, stun guns, door alarms for motels, stun strips, self-defense striking tools, and alarms. The commissions are 25-30% on your sales and 30% on your team's sales. Cost to get started is only $149. Real estate agents who do a lot of work alone in homes on the weekends are great prospects for these products too.

319. **City and Town Researcher**. One of the best websites to check out a new town or city and that will have hundreds of pieces of information about that location is **www.city-data.com**. Put together comparisons of places your clients would like to move to for example, versus where they are currently and you can create a case for a research commission. Besides the personal benefit this site can give you, find ways to use it to build a business online.

320. **Mystery or Secret Shopper**. For many people, the idea of getting paid to shop is a dream come true. There are many mystery shopping scams to beware of, however. Never accept a gig that requires an upfront fee—that's a good sign it's not legit. Legitimate mystery shopping can pay anywhere from $8 per job up to $50 to $100 per job.

Your primary responsibility is to report on your experience. Taking fast food for example, you complete a form provided by the company and report on the QFCS, Quality, Friendliness, Cleanliness and Service) as you order and purchase your food through a drive-thru or at the front counter. You must record the name of your server and submit the form to corporate in 24 hours, along with your receipt for the meal and additional comments about your experience. Companies are willing to pay for your food and $7.00-25.00 for your feedback. **https://bit.ly/2HkeSYJ**. Above is a great example you can check out.

**321. Crime Chart Business**. Produce an audio CD/MP3 or booklet which is about past major crimes in your area. Do research at local libraries and newspaper archives. Have your products stocked at local shops. You might give your CD/MP3 or booklet a title like 'Your Town's Top 30 Crimes'.

**322. Become a Movie or TV Extra**. Depending on where you live, you could become an extra on a TV show or movie. Many studios are always looking for a steady stream of extras, and you can get paid a couple hundred dollars for just standing or walking around in the back of a movie set.

323. **Write and publish a letter about moonlighting**. Give subscribers ideas about moonlighting ventures. Also include articles about subjects such as how to cope with a full-time job, how to manage your income and how to turn a part-time venture into a full-time business.

324. **War Re-Enactment Weekends**. Organize holidays and weekend breaks for those who want to play at being soldiers in World War II or Civil War battles. The games guests play might involve... pursuit, reaching physical objectives, defending positions, obtaining information, etc.

325. **Join or Research or Focus Group**. Have you walked through a college campus and seen the flyer for research studies and focus groups? Companies are always looking for people's opinions about products and services, and for sitting in one of these groups for a few hours, you could earn upwards of $100. Online surveys can net you a regular income as well.

326. **Pool Cleaning Service.** Pool cleaning is another one that can be easy money, as long as you know how to do it. If you don't know where to start, check out online classified ads. There are always existing pool cleaners looking for help with their existing projects and clients. Learn the business and move and start your own. Getting clients is easier than you may think. Few pool owners love to clean their pool and spa. Your enthusiasm and cost and time savings will be all they need to book you.

**327. Snow Shovelling**. In the winter, shovelling snow can be a lucrative side hustle depending on where you live. If you're able bodied, have a truck, shovel, and/or snow blower - you could earn a nice side income. While you used to go door to door and see if your neighbors wanted to pay for your services, there's now an app that can help you find work and get paid. Also put an A-Frame sign out when you're doing someone's yard or driveway and they'll call you! Only drawback is that when the season is over, it's over.

**328. Chain Installer.** Put Chains on and Take off Cars. In the winter where major highways become unpassable because of snowfall, Men and women who install our car chains to get you over the pass and who remove them when it's safe on the other side of the pass. These folks take 4-5 minutes and make $30 per two-wheel install. And then $15 to take them off. Sometimes cars don't have chains, and need to buy them on the mountain, right there. Cost to buy at an auto parts store where you live is about $20-$50. On the mountain, the cost is $100 so definitely come prepared. It's not uncommon for Installers to bring home $1200 a day from the snowy roadways.

**329. Woodworking Weekend.** Begin a business which organizes woodcraft holidays and weekend breaks for those who want to improve and develop woodworking skills. Advertise in woodworking and crafts magazines.

328. **Comedy Still Sells.** Start an online business which sells comedy audio CD's or MP3's. Obtain your stock from comedy audio CD/MP3 publishers. Comedy sells.

329. **Plasma Donation.** This is one of the more interesting ways to make money. You go to your local blood bank or plasma donation clinics and they will pay you a small fee for your blood plasma. It doesn't sounds amazing, but if you need extra money today, this could be a way to earn it. You can expect to be paid anywhere from $20 to $50 per donation.

330. **Participate in Medical Studies.** A unique way to earn you several hundred dollars or more, is being a guinea pig. A recent study that a friend participated in was to get her knees numbed overnight - a different numbing drug in each knee. She then had to tell the doctor which one wore off first the next morning. Odd, but it paid over $1,000 for one night. There are many such studies. Search them out and make good side gig money.

331. **Overtime Work.** If you are working at a job already, this might not be a true side hustle, but it is a way to earn some extra money fast. In many companies, you can volunteer to work longer and earn extra pay. If you don't have an idea on what kind of business to do right now, this could be a good option. I remember when I was younger I would always volunteer for the overtime opportunities. Not only did you get paid well, but you would stand out to your manager, which

would also reward you at review and raise time and would put you first in line for promotions if that's what you want to do.

332. **Employee Referral Program.** Many companies are hiring now. They want new associates that can get along with their current staff too. A great way to earn some extra cash is to refer a fiend to the HR department of your company. Many companies offer referral programs where you can earn anywhere from $50 to $1,000 per employee you refer. That could go a long way. If you know someone who would be a great fit for your company, refer them and see if you can get a bonus for the effort. If your company doesn't have a referral program, suggest one.

333. **Part-time Job**. If you don't want to work for yourself, go spend your time hustling for someone else at a part time job. While not ideal for some, it can be a great way to earn some extra money in your spare time. A server in a restaurant can make an hourly wage and tips. Even in a fast food restaurant at night or at closing, you can make the minimum wage but make it up in the hours that fit your schedule. An extra $600 to $1200 a month or more, can really make a difference in your life.

334. **Make glass display cases designed to a client's requirements**. The display cases might be used for models, stuffed animals or antiques. Advertise in modelling magazines and build up a list of regular clients.

335. **Flower Retailing.** Earn from selling flowers from a table outside your home or on a street corner. Buy stock from a flower wholesalers. Build up a regular base of clients who you can expect to buy a bunch every week from you.

336. **Start a weekly car cleaning and polishing service.** Build up a list of clients by calling on households in your area to promote the service. Employ teenagers, students and fit retired people to do the cleaning and polishing.

337. **Set up an enterprise which organizes the publishing of vanity poetry books.** Poets pay you to have their work published in a professional manner. Each book might contain the work of one or more poets. POD is print-on-demand. It's very popular today. You can publish 125 page book for $2.50-$4.00 Imagine the possibilities? Be a ghostwriter and make $1000-$2000 a book.

338. **Newspaper and Magazine Column.** Devise 'crack the code' quizzes and sell to newspapers and magazines. One example of this type of quiz is a statement where the letters of each word are replaced by different letters of the alphabet. Sell your service to the paper or magazine. Writing a column about the town's news is also a great way to break in to the writing and reporting business.

**339.** **Time Capsules**. Start a service which buries personalized time capsules which contain items from a person's life. Advertise your service in up-market publications. Or start a mail or online service which sells time capsules to people who want to bury things on their property.

**340. Buy A Star Registry.** With the universe as big as it is, research the stars and provide a certificate of ownership for a particular star. For $49.99 you too can own Alpha Centuri. Provide details about the stars that you're selling, their location and why you selected it for them. For entertainment only.

**341. Career Development Weekends**. Organize career selection weekends for teenagers. During these weekends teenagers take aptitude tests, receive counselling and listen to talks about various careers from professionals in those avocations.

**342. Karate Instruction**. Begin a business which produces a series of teach yourself karate videos. Or bring out videos for other martial arts subjects. Sell those videos online. Better yet, if you have a black belt in a particular discipline, start your own karate or taekwondo school. There's big money in teaching martial arts.

343. **Astrology Readings for Babies**. Become an astrologer who specializes in producing charts and readings for babies, children and teenagers. You might, for example, use astrology to provide career advice for teenagers. Do charts and readings by mail and also do personal consultations with parents.

344. **Make cardboard cut-outs of animals for children.** Each cut-out would be six to nine inches high and consist of a photograph or drawing of, for example: an elephant, monkey, tiger or dinosaur. These cut-outs might line a shelf. Package them and sell through shops. Create larger cut-outs for birthday parties that children can stand behind with face cut-outs.

345. **Deal in the antiques and memorabilia of an ethnic group.** Put together a catalog which features: history books, videos, antiques, prints and ephemera. Examples of suitable ethnic groups include: African-Americans, Polish, Italian, West Indian, Scottish, Irish, Native North American, Indian, etc.

346. **Family Crests and Coat of Arms**. Set up a service which reproduces family business of crests, plaques and coats of arms. These might be carved, painted or printed on each plaque. Also offer a design service. Advertise in up-market publications.

347. **Inexpensive Toy Parties**. Have a flea market or craft fair booth which sells inexpensive toys. Demonstrate toys to attract attention. These are very high markup items. Import these for a penny and sell 4 and 5 for dollar.

348. **Insurance Sales.** Insurance licensing is pretty inexpensive and the upside is very high for life insurance, P&C (Property and Casualty- Car Insurance) and final expenses insurance. Want $1000 paydays or more? Insurance brokers are always look going for awesome sales people who are willing to work, sell and learn.

349. **Sell Stock Photos.** Perhaps taking pictures is your forte. If you are a great photographer, you could possibly sell your photos online. Sites like **iStockPhoto.com** are always looking for contributors, who get paid a royalty every time their photo is purchased. This could be a great way to turn your art into some extra cash. Even if you don't like to take pictures, more and more stock photo sites are also looking for digital art and videos as well. If you're strong at creating digital images, you could also consider selling your work.

350. **Design and make fashion clothes** which are tailor-made to an individual's tastes. Advertise your service in trendy publications and place posters everywhere. Place your catalog online so potential customers can find your creations.

351. **Wallpaper Removal**. No homeowner likes to remove old wallpaper anymore. Start a service which specializes in removing and applying wallpaper. Produce a flyer which both describes your first class service and lists your prices. Deliver flyers to households in your area or advertise in the local paper or online at Craigslist.

352. **Take imaginative photographs** of landscapes, cityscapes and people. Enlarge the best of these and frame them. Display at arts and crafts fairs and sell as photographic art.

353. **For Sale Signs**. Design and organize the printing of 'for sale' signs for car owners who want to sell their car. These will have a brightly colored backing and are placed in the car windows by the owner. Arrange for signs to be stocked at car accessory shops. This is not likely a large income type business as consumers can pick up for sale signs in many places today, so make yours unique.

354. **Sell simple exercise equipment** and keep fit devises from your own website. Look to import from Alibaba.com at wholesale pricing. Have it drop-shipped to your customer or to you and you put it together and deliver it for a 2-5 times markup.

355. **Political Postcards & Memorabilia**. Design and produce a selection of satirical, political postcards. Sell sets to collectors, retailers and political activists from ads in political publications.

356. **Basketry Business**. Start a business which designs and manufactures simple basketry kits for beginners. Have them stocked at crafts shops or sell by mail or online in crafts magazines.

357. **Reprint Classics.** Reprint classic photographs and set up a mail or online business to sell these reprints to amateur and professional photographers.

358. **Carve or burn into wood 'I love you' or 'Happy Birthday' messages**. Sell through shops as an alternative to greetings cards. Or sell them from a stall at crafts fairs and markets.

359. **Become a Freelance Photo Journalist.** Get hired on at a network TV news department and volunteer where few like to go. A war zone in a third world country. One idea is to go to one of the many gold rushes around the world and do photo journal reports. One good photo will sell to publications world-wide.

360. **Folk Music Instruments**. Start a business which imports folk music instruments.

Many overseas folk music instruments are made by individuals or small firms who have not considered selling their products in this country. Distribute the imported folk instruments to music shops or sell from your own website.

361. **Bridge Basics**. Put together a course which teaches people how to play bridge. Call your business a school of bridge. Advertise in up-market publications.

362. **E-Book Publishing**. Amazon is the leading E-Book sales platform in the world. Have a story you want to tell? Maybe you should write an eBook and sell them on Amazon or Barnes and Noble. Many authors are making a great full-time income from their books. I've met several authors you've never heard of that sell tons of eBooks on Amazon every year. One author has almost 60+ different books he's selling on Amazon and making $50,000 a month consistently. If you don't want to put together a blog, you could go this route of selling your content online. Blog posts, however, often become tight chapters in an E-Book so consider developing one.

363. **People On-Demand**. Provide people dressed in unusual costumes for promotions. The costume might be specially designed to suit the corporate image of the company. Let advertising agencies and public relations departments know about your service.

364. **Christmas Show**. Start a theatrical enterprise which produces Christmas pantomimes. Do everything yourself, including writing the script, recruiting actors, finding a venue, organizing rehearsals, publicity and selling tickets.

365. **Open a school for hostessing or cashiering**. If a woman or man learns hostessing, serving or cashiering they might as well receive a job in those industries. Your school will teach them to do it properly. Provide a certificate of completion and assist them with job placement as you are able to do so, with business contacts in your local market. Advertise in up-market publications and provide students with a thorough, first class training and watch what happens. If you can provide tuition financing and educational grants for your students, you'll fill your school with anxious new students.

366. **Theme Party Banquets.** Set up a service which organizes theme parties and banquets. The theme for a party might be, for example: medieval, Wild West, 50's, Beach Party or horror. You organize everything for the evening, such as the music, entertainers, costumes, props, waiting staff, food, cutlery, etc.

367. **Magic and Jokes Shop**. Establish an online company which sells magic tricks, jokes and games. Put together you own online catalog and build up a list of regular customers. Your catalog might specialize in one sector of the market such as jokes or magic tricks for children.

368. **Video Pet Business**. Start a business which produces and sells video pets. A person buys a video about a cat or a dog and this acts as a mild substitute for the real thing. The advantages include: no feeding, no smell or hairs around the home, and no looking after or taking out for a walk.

369. **Private Labeled Foot Creams.** With an aging population comes more cases of diabetes and neuropathy. Podiatrists in many areas of the country are just providing surgical services to their patients as they just don't have the time like they used to, for helping patients with prevention. Here's where you come in and can make a patient happy. Provide the best foot creams, water baths and neuropathic pain relievers through a private labeler who will put your name on the bottle and allow you to sell it at pedicure salons and on your website. Brand this for sure and see a very loyal following.

370. **Unusual Products Guide**. Start a business which produces a guide to unusual products, services or shops. Sell by mail order or through bookshops. Also sell advertising space to some of the firms listed in your guide. Use a website or FaceBook fan page to get more subscribers. You decide what kind of unusual products to carry. Make this fun and something your customers look forward too.

371. **Start a special effects rental service.** Hire out machines which make bubbles, wind, fog, falling snow or flashing lights. Your custom will come from private parties, night-clubs, theatres, pop groups and film companies. Also, if required, provide a person to operate the machines.

372. **Civil Service Exam Prep**. Put together a weekend day "Cram-class" so that you can ACE your civil service exam. Cram class would last 4-5 hours and the instructor would reiterate questions and answers quickly and easily so you can better remember the answers. If you are scheduled for your state test, take your cram class on the weekend. If you're scheduled for a Wednesday test, for example, take the cram test Monday or Tuesday as it'll be in your memory longer.

373. **Trade Show Agency**. Create a business which specializes in providing attractive men and women for sales and reception work at business promotions, conferences, trade shows and exhibitions.

374. **Become a Success Consultant or Life Coach.** Earn an income from giving advice on how people can achieve greater success. Start by reaching a clear definition of what your client means by success. Do an assessment of your client's strengths and weaknesses and suggest, for example, a program of changes in approach and career. Put together 6 to 12 month contracts with each new client. Bill in advance or month-to-month.

375. **Rent out real stuffed and mounted birds, fish and other animals.** Your clients might include: restaurants, breweries, clubs, travel agents and other businesses with reception areas. Team up with local taxidermies for best pricing.

376. **Nutritious Dog and Cat Food Recipes**. Dog and cat food is big business today. Write a book which lists recipes for making nutritious dog and cat food and biscuits. Sell to discerning dog /cat owners through pet magazines, pet shops, and your online website. Check out Amazon, Petco and Pet Smart also for ideas.

377. **Become a Real Estate Agent**. Take and pass a real estate test (70% to pass) in your state and become a high paid real estate agent. Join a top real estate company where you will be taught the ropes. You'll learn to take a listing, list it on the MLS (Multiple Listing Service) in your county, sell a home and complete all the paperwork and learn how and what to say to prospective buyers and sellers through your weekly sales training meetings with your broker. How much can you make? Well that depends on you. Of all the realtors in California, the average is $51, 580 a year (as of this publication). Some agents make seven figures annually. It's worth looking into isn't it? And you generally are able to set your own hours.

378. **Pest Control Services**. Learn how to catch, kill and eradicate rodents. When your skill reaches a high standard, go into business for yourself. Get licensed and develop a regular route for your services. Bill monthly. Rodents, ants, cockroaches, fleas, bedbugs and other pest will need to go as well. Your training will help guide you on what you have to do.

379. **Set up a business which invents toys for pets**. Most cat owners love to use cotton, wool, string or paper to play games with their pets. This shows a gap in the market exists. A toy which proves popular with cats has huge sales potential. Also, there is always room for a good new toy for dogs too.

380. **Produce prints of horses and horse racing.** These might be reproduced in a catalog and sold by direct mail or your website or EBay to horse lovers.

381. **Computer and Cell Phone Repair.** If you are skillful with computers and cell phones, you need to be involved with this industry of computer repair.  With the cost of computers coming down and everyone has  at least one computer and a smart phone, keeping them tuned up and running properly is a real challenge, unless you have an honest, skillful and  service minded computer/phone tech standing by.

This is one of the most important people in my life as he has saved me many hours of frustration and hundreds of dollars in outside repair. Be that computer repair person and watch business come naturally and organically to you. Use Craigslist to get the word out about your services along with A-Frame signs on busy streets.

The money is in working with small businesses primarily, who need to make sure that everything runs smoothly every day. Incorporate video surveillance for these companies also as you do installs for them at a fee. Charge these companies $150-$200/month or more as needed. You will save those companies thousands a year. Take on individual computer owners for extra money. For phones, integrate and sync phones with laptops and you'll be busy for a long time.

382. **Make, mount and frame models of butterflies**. The wings are either hand painted or printed. The body of the butterfly might be made of casting metal. The finished model butterflies may be sold through gift or souvenir shops.

383. **Log Furniture and Feeders**. Use logs to make a range of rustic bird tables, nesting compartments and feeders. Have your products stocked at hardware shops, garden centers and online.

384. **Design your own unique brand of cat scratch posts**. Cats are going to scratch. Period. Better on your unique

cat scratch post, instead of on your couch, drapes or sofa. For example, if you have a cat which scratches an armchair or wall, base your design on this. Make, package and distribute your scratch posts to suitable retailers or sell from your website.

385. **Rent-a-Horse Business**. Start a rent-a-horse or pony business. Horse riders, instead of keeping their own horse or pony, rent one from you. Offer horseback riding and lessons on the weekends too.

386. **Dove Releases at Weddings**. Begin a service which provides and releases doves for wedding celebrations and other special occasions. Remember, unless these are trained doves, they aren't coming back. Factor that into your cost.

387. **Set up a dog obedience school**. If you love dogs and appreciate seeing a dog who obeys commands, does tricks and is house broken then this may be for you. Provide residential courses for owners and their dogs. Also hold courses which teach others to become dog obedience teachers. Advertise in both dog and up-market magazines. Dog training is big right now.

388. **Begin an enterprise which organizes day trips to race tracks**. You might, for example, set up a bus service which leaves a city center at a regular time each day and travels to one of the nearby race-tracks open on that day.

**389. Deal in antique and reproduction dolls, and dolls houses**. Build up relationships with collectors so that you know where to sell any new items that you acquire. Also produce a mail or online catalog of reproduction dolls.

**390. Sell PLR, MMR and RR Materials**. Selling the digital products created by another person can be very profitable. For example, **RR** stands for Resale Rights. This means that you have the right to sell the product, as is, for a profit to the end user. You do not have the right to change the product, and you cannot pass on any rights with the product. **MRR** stands for Master Resale Rights, which not only allows you to sell the product, as is, you can pass on the Resale Rights (RR) to the product as well. You still do not have the right to alter the product. **Private Label Rights (PLR)** on the other hand, allow you to change, personalize, or otherwise alter the product to make it into your own, including putting your own name on it as the writer/originator. Once you've determined what you want to sell, being able to find blog articles, books, and even software games is easy. Find your market, find your product and then make the connection.

**391. Casino Bus Trips**. Still a popular excursion for seniors and retired adults, are day trips to Reno, Las Vegas, Atlantic City or an Indian Casino by bus. All travelers meet at a certain place in the morning and return at night.

They purchase a ticket for $25-$30 that takes them up and back and in many cases gives them $10 slot play or $20 match, a $5 food credit for a 5-hour bus stay. See example here. **https://bit.ly/2qQ4VIe.** The bus is always full, but you can relax, read a book or listen to music on the way up and back and game for a few hours when you're there. The casinos provide incentives to bus tour operators as well, to get them there. Can be very lucrative.

392. **Design a log book for cooks.** In this log book a cook records what recipes were tested and comments on the result. Pay to have the log book printed and sell from ads in women's magazines or Amazon.

393. **Network Marketing Done Right**. Decide and then do Network Marketing the right way. It's called the "people's franchise" for a very good reason. The entry into network marketing is very low. $100 to $1000 to be in business unlike the hundreds of thousands for a small franchise. Network marketing makes billions of dollars a year for its representatives around the world...why not you. Find the best network marketing company you can and commit to learning the ins and outs of working with people.

You'll likely start part-time and will move towards full-time as your income increases. MLM (Multi-Level-Marketing), as it's often called, is the number one business in developing true cash millionaires in the world. It's a $200 billion dollar business model today with over 110 million people involved and it's still a growth model that is progressing at 7-10% a year.

Isn't it time to really give MLM a serious look? I've been a part of several network marketing companies over the years and have always felt like I was getting a master's degree in human relations with each one. You will grow personally as well if you plug in and be a part of it. Here's my company. **https://bit.ly/2HTsg2W**

394. **Efficiency Expert Business.** Conduct interviews with the entire staff, including owners. Do your own research to discover what things will improve the business the most. Sell your service .to every business that wants to grow and get improve. Charge $500 a day for your services. Present the final report to the owner of the business on your last day.

395. **Great Composers.** Start a mail or online business which sells books and products related to the great composers. Conduct a world-wide search for products to include in your catalog. Advertise in classical music magazines. Use online social media sites to get the word out.

396. **Start a newspaper clipping service**. Do work for companies who want a comprehensive collection of press clippings about news and developments in their field. Have flyers printed about your service and sent them to firms. As an incentive offer firms a free trial period.

397. **Magnetic Toys for Children & Adults**. Invent and design magnetic toys for children or adults. Ideas for toys include: magnetic building blocks, magnetic picture kits, magnetic puzzles, etc. Pay a manufacturer to make the toys. Get your toys stocked by wholesalers, gift shops and toy shops. Check out whole sites like Alibaba.com.

398. **Top 100 T-Shirt Business**. Start a top 100 chart for witty and artsy T-shirts. Distribute copies of the chart and the top 100 T-shirts to a wide range of retailers. Open your Etsy or Shopify website and promote through Facebook and Instagram. Remember T-shirts are very visual.

399. **Tax Preparation and Money Management Business**. Open and run a school of money-management and tax preparation. Charge tuition to students. Teach students about the techniques, attitudes and systems which can be used for the effective management of money and the preparation of taxes. Students should find the cost of your course more than pays for itself as they can easily find employment for their new found skills.

**400. Test, Test, Test!** Set up an internet business which offers people the chance to do all sorts of tests. Examples of tests might include: IQ, creativity, suitability to be a shop owner or entrepreneur, personality, etc. Pay experts to devise and write the tests for you or see what is already available and tweak it.

**401. Start a dining agency for single people**. Match single people and arrange for them to have dinner dates. Or organize dinner parties for mixed groups. Use ads in local newspapers and singles magazines. Promote also on Facebook and Craigslist.org. There are services today like this that can be tweaked.

**402. Rings for Men.** Bring out a selection of men's rings which feature the name or emblem of popular football or baseball teams. Buy rings wholesale and retail them at fairs and online.

**403. Craft Network Online**. Produce a publication which consists entirely of advertisements from sellers of craftwork and craft equipment and supplies. This online catalog might be like a directory, but instead of displaying the goods of one seller, it contains ads from hundreds of different craft sellers. Make it available to the public for free, and charge craft vendors to be a part of it.

404. **Stamp Collecting Publication.** Start an international advertising publication for stamp collectors. Provide dealers and collectors with an international dimension to their sales efforts and search for stamps. Besides your online website presence, create a FaceBook group fan page too so that collectors can readily communicate with each other and do it more easily.

405. **Local Touring Company**. Set up a firm which provides tours of the best parts of a big city. Your tour might visit: museums, theater and Broadway shows, but also avoiding the skid row areas, and the crime-ridden neighborhoods, etc.

406. **Personalized Print-On-Demand Products**. Produce souvenir pillowcases. Each pillowcase might be printed with pictures of tourist scenery. Souvenir pillowcases have the novel feature that they help a person to relax and sleep because the pictures prompt a person to think of pleasant holiday locations. Open an Etsy or Shopify account and consider using any of hundreds of POD (Print on Demand) service providers that will personalize your pillowcases, mugs and T-shirts. The best part is that it can be setup easily, inexpensively and orders come in and are processed automatically and drop shipped immediately.

**407. Sports Team Memorabilia**. Begin a mail or online business which sells sports team and player memorabilia, videos, photographs, postcards, posters and plaques. Advertise in sports magazines and programs and on Craigslist and from your own memorabilia website.

**408. Assemble and Sell Fossils**. These might be based on a type of animal, for example, insects or fish. Or organize them according to particular geological periods. Sell to collectors and schools.

**409. Start a children's telephone pal club**. Pen pal clubs help children develop their communication abilities. This club helps them to become accustomed to using the telephone. Each member receives introductory notes about the interests of the child he or she will shortly speak to.

**410. Firewood Dealer.** Locate a source of firewood for stoves and open fires. Start a business that packages the wood for distribution to retailers and individuals and delivers the wood directly to them. Hardwoods are best and burn cleaner and longer. Oak, hickory and black locust woods burn hottest and longest. Line up your wholesale source and start placing road signs, and ads on Craigslist for customers. At $130-$200+ a cord there's real money in wood.

**411. Start a semi-professional theatre group** which earns money from performing at private parties, business promotions, tourist sites and public events. Develop your acting skills and make money too.

**412. Weather Art.** Begin a crafts business which incorporates a barometer, digital clock, calendar and thermometer into a single framed picture box. For example, these might be a picture of an aircraft cockpit or cityscape and set among the dials or skyscraper is the barometer, clock, etc.

**413. Leather Phone Holsters.** Develop leather belts and holsters for holding personal stereos and phones. Arrange for these belts and holsters to be stocked at shops which sell records and audio equipment. List and sell them from your website too.

**414. Marketing Manager.** Marketing is the activity, set of institutions, and processes for creating, communicating, delivering, and exchanging offerings that have value for customers, clients, partners, and society at large." In addition to the actual marketing work, marketing managers have the added responsibilities of hiring staff and team building; vision sharing and strategic planning; and managing budgets and tracking their results. The Bureau of Labor Statistics rates this a top 15 job in the US and an average salary of $131,180.

415. **Attention YouTubers!** Creating your own YouTube channel can bring you tens of thousands of dollars monthly. Give your best away in video posts to your subscribers. Entertain and teach them about something or several things, that you're passionate about and then build a huge active subscriber list of 25,000-100,000+ and monetize it. Watch the checks flow in. YouTube viewers want real information in a short video. Do this and see what happens. Cross promote with Facebook friends and Instagram shout-outs and see your team grow. Exciting!

416. **Business Operations Manager**. Business operations managers are the go-to men or women in any business. They help various departments within a company coordinate to meet the company's end goal. Every business needs them, large or small, regardless of industry. Their job includes hiring people, negotiating contracts, addressing budget matters, understanding general business operations and guiding work teams for projects. They also make strategic decisions about what customers are likely to buy and create company policies that help the staff operate efficiently. It's beginning to sound like you? Duties vary widely and depend on the company's needs. Operations really is the heart of most companies, because the operations department actually gets the job that the company needs to get done, done! Become that person in your company or in a mid-large company and expect to be paid a solid six-figure income with all the benefits.

417. **Begin a business which invents, produces and distributes role-playing board games**. This field is not as competitive as other board games and if a game can gain a reputation role-playing game enthusiasts will be willing buyers.

418. **Become a Software Developer**. This is the **#1 job in America** according to US News and World Report.

Software developers are in high demand these days and on average make six-figure incomes. The best software developers are creative and have the technical expertise to carry out innovative ideas. They might spend their days working on a client project from scratch and writing new code. But they could also be tasked with maintaining or improving the code for programs that are already up and running. Software developers also check for bugs in software. And although the job does involve extreme concentration and chunks of uninterrupted time, software developers have to collaborate with others, including fellow developers, management or clients. Developers are often natural problem solvers who possess strong analytical skills and the ability to think outside the box.

419. **SEO- Search Engine Optimization.** For those that have computer knowledge combined with marketing savvy,

SEO, search engine optimization, is every business owners needed service if they operate a corporate website. You see **Search Engine Optimization** or SEO is the simple activity of ensuring a website can be found in search engines for words and phrases relevant to what the site is offering. In many respects it's simply quality control for websites.

Having said that, if there was ever an industry that was little understood by OUTSIDERS its SEO. Get search rankings on page one of Google for a business, it will pay you handsomely, as this reduces your customer's advertising spends. SEO is worth its weight in gold when done properly. Be that individual and see your demand explode.

420. **Living Scriptures**. Put together a company which publishes a living bible on video DVDs. Each DVD might be devoted to a different book of the bible. The bible might be presented by readers and actors, acting out important stories in the Bible. Add scenes from the Bible of various Biblical characters and your production comes to life.

421. **Interior Decoration Business**. Start an interior decoration business which specializes in a particular design. Your service might include fitting ornamental oak beams and providing iron and brass wall ornaments. Put together a sales presentation and advertise in up-market magazines.

422. **Sensory Exploration**. Create an online business which sell sensory exploration kits for young children. Make many of the kits yourself. For example, one kit might consist of addresses a wide range of colors on different cards, another might have a wide range of rough and smooth materials.

423. **Painting Curbs**. Earn money from selling house numbers or painting curbs with the house numbers on the curb. Sell the signs or (painting) door-to-door Houses often have rusty, faded old or difficult to see numbers. This presents an excellent opportunity for a direct sales business. Why it's important is because emergency vehicles can better see your home if needed. Going price to the customer is in the $10-$15 range as of this writing.

424. **House Cleanup Service**. Set up your own furniture removals business and after move-out cleanups. Start by renting a van or truck to do the removals and if business proves promising, buy your own van or tuck and contact every realtor and real estate investor in town with what you do. Print up cards and flyers. Find a local Real Estate Investor's Club and introduce yourself as the home cleanup expert in your area.

425. **Be the CD/MP3 DVD Expert.** Create a trade publication for publishers of audio CD's, DVDs and MP3's.

This publication should give the latest news about the industry. Also accept ads from businesses who want to sell products to audio CD/DVD/MP3 publishers and producers. Purchase a CD/DVD Duplication machine and make copies for local customers.

426. **Penny Stock Advisor.** Imagine buying 10,000 shares of a penny stock for .10 cents and have it go to 1.00? Imagine the thrill? Wouldn't it be great to be on the cutting edge of new industry and business development? Write and publish an annual directory about 'penny stocks'. Every investor will want their copy. The purpose is to examine the performance of penny shares companies over the past year. Sell by direct mail to investors, have stocked in bookshops and advertise in investment magazines. Get security licensed to avoid any legal issues.

427. **Start a school of stock market investment.** With the number of shareholders growing there is a growing demand for learning about investing in the stock market. Hold classes at home and in offices and halls. Also do an investment course or a lesson of the month letter. Get securities licensed of course. Teach Day-Trading at a high level.

428. **Start a business which produces water proof periscopes for viewing things underwater.** For example, at the seaside, or at a lake, a person on the surface can put the periscope into the water and look around underwater.

429. **Sell ideas and recipes for making unusual cakes**. For example cakes shaped like: cars, UFOs, trains, ships, famous landmarks, etc. For each design produce a folded page, like a knitting pattern. Sell these printed patterns through outlets which sell cake decorations.

430. **Make pendants from sea-shells.** Use gold paint to highlight the features of each shell. Or use ordinary paints for pictures or patterns on each shell. Sell through gift or souvenir shops or from a market stall.

431. **Seek out the most powerful magnifying glass in the world.** Buy numerous of these at trade prices and start a mail or online business with your product as the 'World's Most Powerful Pocket Magnifying Glass'.

432. **Making Money with Photography**. Write and publish a blog and create a course for those who want to make money with their photographic or video camera. In each issue give a detailed description of a selected enterprise. Also provide subscribers with other money making ideas and news and tips about photography and video making.

433. **Gold and Silver Plating**. Set up a mail or online business which gold plates anything the customer wants. You can also silver plate too. Use creative advertising to put across your sales message. Post cards and direct mail to auto shops

and car dealerships and head shops, home of unique merchandise and services.

**434. Enameling Craft Business.** Create your own online catalog which is devoted to enameling craft equipment and supplies. You can commission manufacturers to make many of the supplies.

**435. Jewelry Retail Rack**. Place racks of bead necklaces, earrings, bracelets and other jewelry creations at a wide range of shops. Buy the jewelry from importers and mount them on the racks yourself.

**436. Buy and Sell Small Businesses**. At some point in a business owner's life, they decide to retire and sell their business. Write and publish a book about how to get the most money from selling your small business. Sell this to small business owners through Amazon or via postcard targeting small businesses.

**437. Diet and Exercise Programs.** This is a huge business opportunity for those with some knowledge of diets, exercise, health and nutrition. Sell figure improving aids and techniques from your website. For example, you might sell exercise programs, or products which help to remove tummy bulges or excess fat on legs.

Sell successful products already on the market through an affiliate program and make 50-75% commissions. There are dozens of these programs at places like Clickbank.com.

438. **Indian Clothing**. Design and manufacture kits for making moccasins and other Indian apparel. These kits could be the basis of a mail order or online program. Advertise in publications read by young adults and craft magazines.

439. **Craft Business How-To Source**. Write and publish a series of manuals about starting and running a variety of different crafts businesses. Examples of crafts covered might include: leatherwork, soft toy making, pottery, woodcarving, and vinyl craft work. Sell through classified ads or have stocked in craft shops. Also use Craigslist and other free classified websites.

440. **Sales Letter Marketing**. Start a business which specializes in writing sales letters. Call on small businesses to sell your service and show samples of your work. Your service should be good enough to improve the sales pull of almost any sales letter a firm already has. Double their sales with your marketing letters and materials, and you'll be a staff member soon. Remember, sales cure all ills. If not all, about 99% of them for sure!

441. **Produce a cataloging system for record and CD collectors.** This system might consist of a card index box with pre-printed index cards. Each card has a printed section for the name of the artist, record and record label. Sell this cataloging system through shops or develop a software program to keep track and organize. Perhaps even a phone app could be the new answer for keeping your music organized.

442. **Invent and develop a program which is designed to turn the downtrodden soul into a successful person.** The program might take the form of a series of booklets or loose-leaf binders of information, or course. Topics can include time management, developing your positive expectancy mindset, learning to be a real communicator, selling yourself in any situation etc. Sell your program from ads in newspapers, magazines and of course your own internet website.

443. **Take top quality photographs of historic and well-known buildings in your town or region.** Select the best photographs and have these printed on writing paper and envelopes. The idea is that tourists will use this stationery to write home. Also do the same for other towns or regions.

444. **Design a range of first name self-adhesive stickers for** children to put on their books or toys. Sell through toy shops and your business website.

**445.** **Bring together a selection of books and CD's or MP3's about self-hypnosis** and start a mail or online business. Produce a catalog about your products and send it to those interested in astrology, the occult and self-improvement.

**446. Make & Teach Toy Making.** Learn how to make soft toys with the long term objective of being able to earn money from teaching others. Eventually, teach solo students, classes or use diagrams to teach people from your YouTube channel and your website's vlog. Also begin a course teaching people how to design their own soft (quiet) toys.

**447. Make a selection of children's prayer plaques.** Wooden wall plates which feature popular prayers. The prayers might be painted onto or burned into the wood.

**448. Make vinyl stickers and sell them on Etsy and EBay.** These stickers have many uses and can be marketed lots of different ways. Imagine creating a 9" x 9" vinyl biblical verse sticker for a 12" x 12" decorative tile that is hung on your wall or placed on a book holder. The imagine charging $30-$40 for it. Cost of vinyl…$1.00. Cost of Tile $2.00. Are you getting the picture here? Vinyl cutting machines can be acquired for $250 or so. You'll need rolls of vinyl also.

**449. Writing Your Autobiography.** Produce a course about how to write your autobiography. Biography publishing

Is a large sector of the book industry today. Create questions to be answered for any good autobiography. Write your own autobiography first. Get it printed at www.lulu .com and give or sell to your family members. Advertise your service for a flat fee or hourly rate.

450. **Old Print Framing**. Cut out prints and illustrations from old books. Frame them and sell to a wide range of shops and from a stall at a market fairs and car boot sales.

451. **Comics Supplier**. Set up a business which sends American comics to both expatriates and overseas collectors of comics. You might send comics on a weekly basis as they are published, save them up and post every quarter or advertise world-wide offering a sample of American comics. Always give credit to the original comic creator.

452. **Role Playing Games.** Start a site for role-playing game enthusiasts and or video game players. In each post give subscribers: tips about how to win games, cheats, review new games, act as a forum for discussion about games. Teach the basic of the "Who Done it Murder Mysteries." Sell space to display and classified advertisers. Use Facebook and game rooms to invite new players.

**453. Produce a series of Whodunit audio CD's or MP3's**. Get your CD's or MP3's stocked at bookshops and build up a reputation for producing the best whodunit CD's or MP3's. Alternatively, produce a series of adult whodunit CD's or MP3's. They can be sold by mail order.

**454. Motto Creation Software or Book.** Publish a booklet which provides a lengthy list of mottos for use by: societies, clubs, institutions, families and individuals. Have the booklet stocked at shops. Also start a website service which devises mottos. Use a page in the booklet to advertise your website eservice.

**455. Research Analyst**. Provide yourself with a regular income by becoming a "research company" selling odd and unusual facts to all kinds of publications and even individuals. For example, sell financial facts to financial magazines, football facts to football program publishers, photography facts to photography magazines, etc.

**456. Disappearing In America.** Bring out a series of booklets or CD's or MP3's about how to get rid of, or escape the attentions of various types of people in society such as: unsatisfactory employers, salesmen, criminals, fools, unwanted stalkers, officials, etc. Sell the books or CD's or MP3's as a complete set online or through bookshops. **EdenPress.com** would be a good example of this.

457. **Fairy Tales.** Produce and distribute an audio CD/MP3 library of fairy tales. Put together a comprehensive collection of fairy tales. Sell online as a complete library or start a monthly club. Advertise in women's and children's magazines.

458. **Local Labor Broker.** Be a broker for local labor that is needed by homeowners in your community. Interview, screen and hire electricians, plumbers, carpenters, yard and home cleanup workers, tree and hedge trimmers, maids, mechanics, grass and landscapers on a 1099 form. Negotiate and pay these professionals the pre-approved rate that you've agreed to work with them on, and charge the homeowner 20-25% more as your fee for connecting them together. You collect the money before the job starts. If there are parts involved, the laborer will report back and you will collect that from the homeowner. With a list of professionals working by the job or by the hour, you can make a real living as a labor broker.

459. **Start a universal correspondence club**. This club should be able to boast that it can find safe individuals to correspond with about any subject. Produce a flyer and website landing page about your club and list many subjects. Recruit club members by placing classified ads in a diversity of publications at home and abroad. Screen them properly.

460. **Become a Freelancer** by working on a contractual basis with your customers through your association with Elance.com, Upwork.com, Fiverr.com and Odesk.com. Visit these websites and signup if you have skills that are marketable. You'll need to put together your credentials (skills) do that potential clients can see how you'll fit into their business plan. Do a great job and get more clients. You'll get jobs by posting a response to client requests and beating out the other contractors. You can make serious money from all around the world. Check it out.

461. **Restaurant Server.** Working as a server is a great second job. Positions also as a host or hostess job can be good also and easier. If you're outgoing and friendly, can manage the guest flow if the restaurant doesn't take reservations, and can juggle phone calls while you're doing other tasks, this is an option to consider. Servers typically will make minimum wage on the hours they work, but also, in a nice dinner house can pull in an additional $10-$25 an hour or more. Breakfast restaurants also be nice but tips aren't as high typically and traffic is generally a little slower. All depends on the restaurant and the town or city you're in. Learning the menu is generally pretty easy too. Many restaurants are hiring. Give this one a shot if you'd like to make $30,000 to $50,000 a year. The work is a little stressful and you're on your feet a lot, but if love people, they will reward you with tips.

462. **Publish a newsletter about the changing English language**. The contents would provide information about new words and meanings. Sell subscriptions to writers, academics, advertising agencies and others who might be interested in new words. English as a second language is big business around the world with companies willing to educate their workers and pay those with an English background and bachelor's degree to benefit financially.

463. **Guitar and Piano Lessons**. Give lessons in your own home to those who want to learn to play the piano or guitar or other instruments you are proficient to teach. There is a vast pool of clients as most people would like to become more musical. Use local advertising and social media to attract students.

464. **Publish a newsletter for separated and divorced people**. Discuss issues relevant to being separate or divorced. Also include classified listings of people who are looking for new partners.

465. **Map Your Town**. Commission an artist to do a contemporary map of your town or region in the style of maps from antiquity. Produce and frame prints of this map. Distribute to shops throughout the region.

466. **Singing Lessons.** Develop a course of singing lessons. If others find your voice pleasing to listen to earn money from singing at events. Teach others to sing, breathe properly, read music and use their talent to make money or teach others.

467. **Stencil Craft**. Begin an online business which sells stencil craft. Make stencils which can be used by woodworkers, painters and craft people; for example, to add attractive designs to their work or walls. A stencil might depict flowers and a woodworker would use paint or ink to imprint the design onto their work.

468. **Street Craft Worker.** Become a street or market craft worker. Sit at your booth making, for example, jewelry, ornaments from wire or shells, or personalizing the things you've made for customers. Display the goods you make at your booth. The act of hand-making the ornaments or jewelry attracts the curiosity of those attending the event. This could result in a respectable level of sales.

469. **Carpet & Upholstery Cleaning.** Buy carpet cleaning equipment and begin cleaning rugs, upholstery, and carpets in customer's homes or businesses. Promote business door-to-door with flyers for "spring cleaning" promo to start. Build a route of dozens of customers quickly and relatively inexpensively. Approach businesses with a similar offer and schedule your work with them every quarter.

470. **Personal Affairs Consultant.** Start a general problem solving service for personal affairs. This service acts like a private "Ask Amy" column. An expert is provided to deal with the problem your client is trying to solve. The expert might give advice by telephone, via Skype or in person. Sell you services to individuals, or approach a number of newspapers in your area for a column in their paper.

471. **Stained Glass Windows**. Learn the art of making stained glass windows. Use your newly acquired skills to earn money from: 1) Teaching people in your own home town your skill, 2) Holding courses at bed and breakfast houses out of season, 3) holding classes in a quiet corner or back room of an arts and crafts shop. Sell your service to local churches, bed and breakfast hotels etc.

472. **Local Entertainment Agency**. Start an agency which supplies entertainers to bars, restaurants and local events. The entertainers might include disc jockeys, musicians, singers and actors. Put a contract together with them and become their agent for 15%. Visit your attorney and create a talent agency document that will allow you to represent your talent to the market. Advertise for entertainers to put on your books, then advertise for business. Join the Chamber of Commerce in nearby towns too and interact with the business men and women who run them.

473. **Promotional Videos for Artists.** Make high quality, low budget, and promotional videos for pop groups and solo artists who are just starting out. Advertise your service at music shops and in the music press. When you receive an inquiry, give the potential client a persuasive sales presentation to represent them and provide them with more gigs for a percentage of their gig.

474. **Design Christmas sleigh bells for cars.** Bring a little Christmas cheer to the holiday with sights and sounds. These bells are attached to the exterior of a car. The motion of the car causes the bells to ring, just like sleigh bells. During the Christmas season these bells should add a pleasant seasonal flavor to cars.

475. **Consultant Training**. Develop a training course which teaches people how to become a consultant. This course should deal with every aspect of setting up a successful consultancy.

476. **Spoken Word Audios**. Put together a mail or online catalog of spoken word audio CD's or MP3's. Canvass audio CD/MP3 publishers to see how they can be of help to you. Place as many audio CD/MP3 titles in this catalog as possible to give potential customers the widest possible choices.

477. **Arcade Game Rental**. Begin a business which hires out second-hand pin-ball machines and computer arcade games to householders. These machines might also be hired out by the night to private parties. Another concept is a large game van for birthday parties with enough game units for 10-12 gamers with every popular game possible. Rent the van out for 4 hours for $400. Invite all your friends and have a blast.  Set these up every week around your area.

478. **Start a children's audio CD/MP3 of the month club**. The records and CD's or MP3's sold by the club might be educational, stories or music. Ask libraries to hang your flyers. Also use Craigslist and other cheap or free websites to promote your "children's audio of the month" program.

479. **Establish a directory of products no longer made**. This directory might include sections on toys, novelties, car parts and household goods. Design the directory for business people and inventors who want to know both what has been made before and what ideas might be revived and/or modified. Fund it with advertising.

480. **Vanity Poetry.** Produce vanity poetry audio CD's or MP3's or videos. Pay a celebrity to read a poet's work to a video camera, or make a recording on audio tape. Your service might also include producing copies of the recording on audio or video CD's or MP3's for distribution. Imagine Morgan Freeman reading your poetry?

481. **Music Business**. Write Amazon books or produce audio CD's or MP3's about different aspects of making a career in the music business. For example: 'How to be an independent record producer', 'How to get a recording contract', 'How to form your own group', etc. Use small ads in the music press to attract buyers or advertise with Google Adwords or use Amazon itself to promote your work. If you can video interview music producers for example, you may have a video that you can market and sell as part of the course.

482. **Subliminal Audios/Videos.** Create subliminal audio recordings on CDs, DVDs or MP3 that help you with your ability to overcome fear, overcome rejection, increase your ability to sell better, stop smoking, stop drinking and other ways to develop your skills or break habits. Create an online catalog and promote on Craigslist and free classified sites to start.

483. **Open a television and video production school.** Organize practical courses in television, radio, podcast and video production. Buy a second-hand closed circuit television system, rent or lease an office or room at a library initially, and use this as the beginning of the school. Teach all you know and research what you need to do to help your students succeed in TV-Radio & Podcasting production.

**484. Start a complete music lessons business.** Offer to tutor potential students in popular musical instruments. Call your agency a school of music. Employ other musicians for other instruments, by taking a 30-50% cut of their lessons for students you've provided to them. Start by using advertising to recruit both part-time tutors and pupils. Don't just offer piano and guitar lessons, when you can offer harp instruction, violin, trumpets, and horns and percussion instruments too?

**485. Tour with the Band or Team.** Begin a business which organizes trips to rock and pop concerts, and football and college sports events. Your service obtains the tickets and provides a bus or minivan to take fans to the venue. Get paid in advance by those who will be attending.

**486. Design and make fashionable clothes for children.** You might sell them direct or through a party plan. Import clothing from Alibaba for example inexpensively and sell it through your Etsy or Shopify store.

**487. Use soft toy materials to make a puppet-like toys which gives children their medicine.** A small soft toy has a clip attached to one hand. A parent puts the spoonful of medicine into the clip and controls the hand so that it appears that the puppet is giving the medicine. Sell by mail or online or through ads in women's magazines.

488. **Become a tutor**. If you're a college student, parent or teacher, tutoring jobs in your area of expertise are a way to make extra money without a long-term commitment. For most jobs, you may need an academic background in the subject matter you wish to tutor but not necessarily. You'll also need patience and excellent communication skills though. Tutoring a student in math or English can bring $15-$25/hour or more depending on complexity and subject matter. Advertise on college job boards, Craigslist and other free classified sites.

489. **Handmade Desktop Stands**. Use wood to make desktop stands for holding reference books such as dictionaries, trade directories, map books and telephone directories. Have these stocked at bookshops and stationers or sell by mail order. Wood is always more elegant than plastic, right?

490. **Learn machine quilting and knitting**. Once your skill has reached a high standard, earn money from teaching others to use knitting machines. Teach people in your own home or theirs.

491. **Make energy saving 'sausages'**. Fill a sausage shaped bag with sand so that it can be placed against a draughty door or window. Sell door-to-door or have them sold in hardware shops. Also sell kits by mail or online. Make the designs fashionable too. Perhaps a cat or dog shape for animal lovers.

**492. Design and make old fashioned country curtains.** Display your curtains on a roadside stall near a busy shopping center in a similar fashion to the way double-glazing or shower firms sometimes display their products.

**493. Gay and Lesbian Community Online Mall.** Set up an online business which serves the gay and lesbian community. In your catalog include suitable: Books, audio CD's or MP3's, videos, novelty products, posters, contact advertising section too, t-shirts, etc.

**494. Wall Hanging Décor.** Begin a service which organizes the production of wall hanging tapestries for a commission. Sell your service to businesses which might want a tapestry of their logo, for example, hanging in a reception area. Or do a style tapestry representing business achievements.

**495. Tax Preparation Business.** It's often said that there are two certainties in life...death and taxes. Why not setup a tax preparation business, to handle one of the most difficult things that we all go through every quarter or every year...taxes? Preparers make $30-$60k a year and generally have flexible hours. Handling business's quarterly taxes during the year, can make it a year round business. Learning the tax business is easy too. H & R Block, Liberty Tax and other companies are always looking to hire tax preparers every year.

In California for example, **www.libertytax.com** requirements for passing the tax course are attending the 60-hours of training and passing each exam with a score of 70% or above. This can be classroom or online. The live online courses will be held Tuesday and Thursday from 6-9 p.m. PST beginning Tuesday, beginning August each year. If you are unable to attend the live events, you may still register for this course and follow the replays of the classes at your convenience. The cost is $239.00, which covers the cost of associated materials for the tax course. A great gig for those that love number-crunching and helping their clients get refunds.

496. **Be the T-Shirt Mogul**. Bring out a range of T-shirts to distribute to segments of the population. For example, target real estate investors, moms, dads, golfers, fishermen, and workout and gym goers. The design on the T-shirts might be aimed at the customers of these professions or other interests too. Use POD (Print-On-Demand) suppliers so that you can print them one by one and not have to print hundreds at a time. This is the greatest discovery for t-shirt marketers ever! Setup your Shopify store and learn this business. You'll be rewarded nicely if you also learn how to market and drive traffic to your site.

**497. Boxers or Briefs?** Have an undergarments market booth and sell: men's and women's underwear, socks, tights, stockings, leggings, fancy lingerie, long johns, etc.

**498. Produce magnetic perpetual calendars.** A strip of metal is printed with day numbers and the names of months. Two magnetic markers are used to indicate the date. Personalize those calendars and get $20-$25 for them.

**499. Design and manufacture kits for making clothes.** The kits might be aimed at those who have basic sewing skills, but would need a kit if they want to make something a bit more complex. Produce a catalog about your kits and advertise in women's magazines and online at places like Craigslist.

**500. Start a scarf or accessory club.** Each month or quarter club members automatically receive one of the latest fashionable accessories selected by the club. Your club might have a single annual membership charge. Membership would make an ideal gift. Creating quality work will sell them more easily.

**501. Gay and Lesbian Short Stories.** Produce books or audio CD's or MP3's which contain gay and lesbian short stories. Sell them via Amazon or online at your website. Stock them in shops which are used by the gay and lesbian community. Niche marketing.

502. **Set up a home-based computer service** which maintains the mailing lists of local businesses. Also supply local businesses with mailing lists bought or rented from other firms in this country.

503. **Open a computerized marketplace for cars and motorcycles.** On your computer, list the sellers and what they have to sell. Charge the sellers a fee for this service. Place ads which invite people who want to buy a car or bike to telephone you to see if you have what they want.

504. **Begin a business which makes money from souvenir cosmetics**. Bring out lipstick, for example, or hand cream which has a local theme or name. Buy from established cosmetics manufacturers and package under your own private label.

505. **Home Computing Instruction from Home**. If you have the necessary knowledge and skill earn money from teaching home computing in your own home or the home of your clients. Prepare lessons on a variety of popular software applications and general computer operation. Give classes or teach to individual students on individual programs. Perhaps you can focus on the older senior market who have means but very little skill in computer knowledge.

506. **Home Computing For Seniors.** Begin a business which produces courses about home computing.

Base each course on a popular software application and have a general course on general computer operation. The lessons in your course might be modelled on what already exists in textbooks. Sell from ads in computer magazines.

507. **Tour Company**. Organize tours of well-known sights or areas of outstanding natural beauty. Buy or rent an open topped bus for the tours. Also use this bus for weddings, work excursions and school trips.

508. **Design and make a range of fishing lures at home.** Sell these by getting them stocked at local fishing tackle and bait shops, starting a monthly club which sends anglers one of the latest fishing lures and giving the lures an appealing name like 'lucky charm lures'.

509. **Start an online VLOG (Video Blog)** for people who want to make money from their home computer. In each presentation (or podcast) provide subscribers with ideas for adventure games, educational or quiz programs, and business programs. Also print news, tips and case studies about succeeding in your computing business. Create a course that will have all of the benefits of owning and operating an Internet marketing business.

**510. Begin a computing lesson of the month club**. Each month send a home computing enthusiast a CD/MP3/DVD which gives instructions about how to use a popular application or how to improve their programming skills. Advertise in home computing magazines or from Craigslist.

**511. Start a mail or online business which sells mosaic making supplies**. Also sell a guide about getting started in this fun hobby. Produce a simple catalog about your products and advertise in crafts magazines.

**512. Learn the art of tap dancing** and put together your own song and dance act. Find an agent and perform at clubs, bookstores, coffee shops and private functions.

**513. Scrapbooking.** Design and manufacture kits for making paper at home and supplies for scrapbooking. Sell the kits to craft workers from ads in crafts magazines and get them stocked in hobby and crafts shops.

**514. Grief Counselor.** If you've ever lost a loved one, mom, dad, brother, sister, a friend or your own child, you've likely experienced grief of losing them. Preparing people as they go through these experiences is important. Creating a business service is a little trickier but needed.

It helps to have a psychology background (and perhaps a degree) or in being a pastor or minister, and an understanding of dealing with "end-of-life" situations and death and being able to communicate with grieving family members and friends about it. Group or individual counseling could be the answer to help your clients experience grief and get back to their lives with confidence. Promote your service to funeral homes, churches and even cemeteries.

515. **Produce a rhyming dictionary** on audio CD's or MP3's. A spoken word dictionary can illustrate the rhyming qualities of words far better than any printed dictionary. Get these stocked at bookshops or sell from adverts in literary magazines.

516. **Left-Handed Store**. Start a mail or online company which sells business equipment and accessories for left-handed people. Left-handers are about 10% of the US population. Bring out a catalog or online website with all things left-handed. You know you'll have 34 million loyal customers to go after.

517. **Publish a craft workers' equivalent to the 'Yellow Pages'.** In the directory include the addresses of sources for a wide range of products. List the addresses under a heading for each craft. Also sell advertising space to suppliers, crafts schools, craft workers, etc.

518. **Toy Model Rental Agency**. Set up a service which rents out model trains, boats, drones and planes to businesses with reception areas. These models are supposed to create goodwill because most people will look at and appreciate a good model. Your clients will include restaurants and office-based businesses and particularly travel agents. For the more active approach, and for those with several drones, for example, have the guests do some drone racing after being taught how to use them. Very fun for attendees of an event.

519. **New but Soiled Shop**. Canvass shops for older, soiled or other unwanted stock and offer to buy it at a discount. No one else is likely to buy the stock so this is probably the only opportunity the owner has to sell it. Have a yard sale and sell the stock at low prices to the public.

520. **Reprint old geographical maps.** Use the reprints to decorate unfinished stock bought from manufacturers and then sell. For example: desk sets, book ends, memo pads, letter racks, lamp holders, book ends, coasters, dinner mats, etc. Alternatively frame the maps in a stylish frame and sell as wall decorations.

521. **Bags of Coins**. Package low value foreign coins in small collector's plastic bags. Distribute these coins to comic stores for selling to children in the way small packets of stamps are sold. Advertise online too on your own website.

**522. Drawing and Etching Kit**. Start a firm which manufacturers kits for making etchings. Also teach other how to etch and paint. Design the kits so that a complete beginners can make attractive etchings and paintings. Sell by mail or online or through shops which sell artists' materials.

**523. Beers From Around the World.** Put together a dozen bottles of beer from breweries around the world. Market them through warehouse club stores, major retailers, and from your own website. Buy wholesale and sell to retailers. Brokerage fees if necessary.

**524. Beadwork Business**. Set up a bead craftwork business. Use beads to make a selection of Jewelry such as necklaces, pendants, bracelets and earrings. Sell from a market stall or mount on display racks and get shops to stock them.

**525. Commemorative Wall Plaques**. Start a business which makes a range of souvenir or commemorative wall plaques. They might have a feature such as: town crests, tourist maps, commemorative statements or logos, etc. Sell your wall plaques through gift shops, drug stores, local retailers and hotels.

**526. Home Scaffolding Rentals**. Rent out scaffolding for exterior home decorating and maintenance. Advertise in local newspapers and newsagents windows. Provide a free delivery service.

527. **Advanced Driver Safety Class**. Bring out an audio CD/MP3 course about advanced driving. Sell by mail or online or get it stocked in bookshops. Or produce videos about improving driving skills and hire or sell by post. Each video might feature filmed examples of good or bad driving.

528. **Personalized Jigsaw Puzzles.** Set up a business which produces personalized jigsaw puzzles. Photos of children on the jigsaws make this fun and personal. These might be sold either by mail or online.

529. **String Puppets**. Design and manufacture kits for making string puppets. Produce a selection of kits which are complementary to each other and can be used in the same puppet show.

530. **China Dolls**. Learn how to make china dolls and once your work reaches a high standard make an income from teaching others or selling the dolls you make. Hold classes in your own area or devise a course on how to do it.

531. **Make Personalized Peg Calendars**. A peg calendar consists of a block of wood with a line of 31 holes for days, 12 holes for months, and 10 holes for years. Three tiny pegs indicate the date and are moved each day accordingly. The calendar can hang from a wall like a thermometer or sit on a desk. The personalization comes with a vinyl strip.

**532. Caricature Drawing Artist**. If you can draw amusing caricatures of people you've got a job for life. Do this for people at fairs, flea markets, bazaars and events. Draw one on the spot and charge $10-$15 or so for each one. Sell a complimentary frame if you like too as an add-on.

**533. Re-Create Old Baseball or Cigarette Cards**. Arrange for a set of pictures to be printed to look like old cigarette or baseball cards. Turn out hundreds of framed sets and sell to wholesalers and gift shops.

**534. Draw amusing cartoons of personal names** at any location where there are crowds, for example: fairs, trade shows, shopping areas and tourist sites. It's a novel idea and event organizers will appreciate your talent.

**535. Artists Yearbook**. Who are these talented people? Create a year-book for people who do creative things with their hands, such as painters, drawers, sculptors, cartoonists, illustrators, cartoonists, engravers, etc. Also list buyers of art, art schools, art fairs, etc. Have the year-book stocked at bookshops, artist's supplies shops, craft shops and sell online.

**536. Sketch Artists School**. Start a training school which specializes in teaching the art of sketching. Use sketch artists to do the teaching. Your job is to find students and organize the premises and management. Also put together an artist course which teaches sketching to beginners.

537. **Finger-Painting Kits for Kids**. Design and manufacture finger painting kits for children and adults. Get these stocked at shops which sell toys (for children's kits) and artists materials (for adult's kits). Sell online too.

538. **Market research analysts and specialist**. Research market conditions and create marketing campaigns for businesses on a contract basis or working for a company. Creativity and a flair for expressing it through marketing and advertising vehicles is a real plus. Median pay $61,290.

539. **City's Cartoon Mascot.** Invent a cartoon character which captures the spirit of your town or region. Pick a name which matches the name of the town or region. E.g. Billy Brighton, Mickey Middlesex, etc. Use this character on: T-shirts, posters, postcards, stationery, mugs, flags, etc.

540. **Wine wholesaling.** Make money from wines by taking an empty van to a wine growing region and bringing it back full. Sell the wine directly to restaurants, off licenses, and free houses. Build up a list of business who will buy wine from you on a regular basis. Check state and local laws first.

541. **Private Label Nutritional Supplements**. If you love nutritional supplements and can tell stories about how they have helped you and others, perhaps you should be developing a private label line of your own nutritionals.

Market to problems that people have. Brand your line. Make sure your manufacturer makes only the highest quality products available from the best ingredients. Cheap nutritionals aren't what you want to put your name on. Sell online at Amazon.com, Craigslist, and your own website. Use social media to spread the word too. Testimonials are key to product branding and development. Get lots of them.

**542. Take Wine Tours.** Specialize in organizing trips to vineyards and beer festivals. Issue an annual or quarterly brochure which gives full details of all the holidays you are planning. Advertise in beer and wine publications.

**543. Sell plans for hobby electronic construction projects.** Buy plans from established electronics hobbyists and compile a catalog of plans for sale. Find and sell plans through adverts in electronic hobby magazines.

**544. How-To-Book Development.** Begin a party plan business which sells self-instruction and 'how to' books, CD's or MP3's and courses. Add a competitive edge to the business by producing many of the products yourself.

**545. Hobbies to Business.** Write and publish a series of booklets on how to turn various hobbies into businesses, for example, 'How to start an electronics business'.

Other hobbies might include: stamp or book collecting, photography, angling, and video making. Sell through ads in hobby and business opportunity magazines.

**546. Love Connection**. Produce a questionnaire which is designed to find out if one person really loves another. Place classified ads in magazines for teenagers or women which read: 'Does he really love you?' Or, "Is he really into you?" Send respondents a questionnaire and process it for a charge. Or design a questionnaire which can be assessed by the client.

**547. Create a Yoga School**. Yoga is a group of physical, mental, and spiritual practices and disciplines which originated in ancient India. There is a broad variety of yoga techniques. Focus on what is popular in your area and give the best service and instruction possible.

**548. Home Music Study Program**. Produce and sell from national publications a home study course about how to play the piano or guitar. Pay an expert pianist and guitarist to devise and write your course. Check out affiliate programs that are already done for this training and tap into their teaching and receive a 50-75% affiliate commission from your website by simply driving traffic to your site.

**549. Make a series of cookery instruction videos**. These should teach people how to make all kinds of unique dishes and foods. Start a business to sell these videos.

**550. Boat Trips and Bus Excursions**. At a seaside resort set up a seasonal business which organizes boat trips and day-long coach excursions for holiday-makers. The boat and buses will be hired from local operatives and you can sell tickets from camping site shops, local retailers and tourist information centers.

**551. Exam Techniques**. Devise and produce an audio CD/MP3 course about successful exam techniques. An important selling point is that anyone with average intelligence can pass most exams if they know about exam techniques.

**552. Print stationery with a thematic design for hobbyists**. For example, photographers can have writing paper and envelopes printed with pictures of cameras, films and lights. Get this stationery stocked at hobby shops and sell by mail or online through the appropriate hobby magazines.

**553. Reducing Employee Turnover**. Turnover is a fact of life in business, but you can dramatically reduce it with tips and running a good operation. Compile and publish a guide for employers throughout the country who have high staff turnover. Turnover costs employers dearly every year. SHRM states that every time a business replaces a salaried employee, it costs 6 to 9 months' salary on average.

For a manager who earns $40,000 a year, that's $20,000 to $30,000 in recruiting and training expenses. Employers are always looking for new employees to hire. Sell copies of this guide to job hunters and managers through bookshops, classified ads, Craigslist or Amazon in the form of an ebook or paperback. Keep information updated each year. Another avenue would be to put be to put on turnover seminars for restaurants, and corporations. Teach managers how to reduce this business killing expense.

554. **Design and manufacture portable mini-golf courses**. Each hole on the course might consist of a large, colorful wooden sheet which has pop-up features like a pop-up book. Nine sheets will fit in a van. Sell or hire for fund raising and money-making events.

555. **Money Belts**. Use various fabrics to make money belts of your own design. Attach each money belt to a printed card and sell these fully stocked to shoe repair shops and newsstands.

556. **Design and make wooden wheels of fortune.** Produce in a variety of sizes and designs. Sell or hire as fund-raising aids to clubs, associations, schools and colleges.

557. **Sales Training.** Produce an audio CD/MP3 training course about salesmanship. The object of the course might be to bring out and develop the salesperson in anyone. For this

reason almost everyone is a potential buyer. Sales and closing are million dollar skills that are transferable to any business. As you can learn and cultivate your sales skills, you can literally work anywhere for anyone and make a great living. Sales is still one of the top professions in the world.

**558. Cookies & Chocolate.** Sell home-made cookies, chocolates, and sweets via classified ads or from your website that you've created. The products made should be of highest quality that can be sold either from a booth or to colleagues, friends and local businesses.

**559. Gaming and Lottery Authority**. Conduct your own research into the subject of how to make money from gaming and slot machines, gambling and lottery systems. Write and publish a book about your findings. Research all of the systems in the market. Sell from classified ads, direct mail and website. Emphasize that people could make a lot of money from buying your research.

**560. Winning!** Start an online business that sells books about how to win at gambling. The games covered might include: roulette, baccarat, poker, keno, slot machines and horse-racing. Sell your book direct through your website and offer it at Amazon as an Ebook and paperback. Expand to Barnes and Noble and other online bookstores.

**561. Teach Yourself Texan!** Produce a series of audio CD's or MP3's which give instruction about how to mimic different accents. For example: 'Teach yourself to speak like a Texan'. Other accents might include: Yorkshire, cockney, French, English, Scottish, New York, and Valley Girl etc. Especially important for actors and actresses and those in theater productions. Have fun with this. It'll provide you with tons of publicity too. Just do it.

**562. Amusing Message for Plants**. Have amusing messages printed in speech bubbles on the sides of potted plant holders. For example: Hello, my name is...', 'Shake my water, don't stir it', 'Please Sing to Me This Morning', etc. Have these stocked at outlets which sell garden products.

**563. Tree Growing**. Put together a kit for growing trees from seeds or by sending small pine trees, lemon trees, etc. In each kit include instructions about how to get the best results. Sell from ads in gardening publications or through suitable shops. Always sell through your website as well and thus eliminating a middleman. What's the best time to plant a tree? 20 years ago. The next best time...is now.

**564. Hydroponics Gardening.** Begin a mail or online business which sells **hydroponics** growers supplies (hydroponics is a method of growing plants without soil).

One of the biggest reasons hydroponics has become so popular is because recent studies on hydroponic farming have shown it to have many benefits. Plants grown hydroponically are of exceedingly high quality, occupy less space, and consume fewer resources than traditional growing methods. Additionally, hydroponic growing methods, in combination with vertical gardening, have aided in expanding the possibilities of urban gardening and indoor gardening. Produce a catalog and advertise in gardening publications.

565. **From the Beaches of the World**. Obtain quantities of sand from the beaches of the D-day invasion. Place the sand in tiny bottles and sell world-wide as souvenir sand from the beaches of the 1944 D-day invasion. Add a name label to each bottle to show which beach the sand came from. Sand from the sunny California beaches as well as other famous places.

566. **Garden Hammocks**. Start a business which makes garden hammocks. Devise your own hammock which has at least one superior feature over other hammocks available. Sell through hardware shops and garden centers and by mail or online from ads in gardening publications.

567. **Wishing Wells.** Use logs and wood to make small ornamental garden wishing wells. Sell through garden centers and hardware shops and from your front yard and website. People will them in your driveway and want one.

568. **Hair Jewelry**. Create a line of hair jewelry. This could be made from real or artificial human hair and is knotted like dreadlocks. The Jewelry also includes colored beads in the design. The result is dreadlocks necklaces, brooches and earrings as well.

569. **Massage Therapist.** Earn your Certified Massage Therapist license, and earn money on the side doing massages and working out knotted muscles. You may be able to get part-time shifts at a local health club or work as an independent contractor through a local massage studio. You can earn nearly **$60 per hour**, according to **Payscale**.com and local massage therapists. There are many different massage techniques and modalities. Learn what sells best and branch out from there. There are Swedish massages. Hot stone, aromatherapy massage, deep tissue and Shiatsu massage as well as Thai, sports massage and even chair massage. There is even pregnancy massage and reflexology. Master these through your massage training and be everyone's best friend for life!

570. **Roadside Flower/Fruit Stand**.  Sell flowers and/or fruit from a roadside stand. Setup a 10'x10' tent and sell from the roadside. There are always folks that will purchase flowers and fruits and vegetables from a stand.

Get these wholesale from farmers and growers and markup to still be a bargain for shoppers. Also, sell single roses from your booth. Put up a big sign which both tempts people to buy a single rose and state the price. Encourage drivers to stop and bring love back to their loved ones.

571. **Become a school bus driver**. They typically work less than 20 hours per week **and** average more than $15 an hour. Apply at your local school district for the position. You should have a good driving record and be current on insurance and licensing. A great part-time gig. Sometimes there's even benefits too.

572. **Start a venture which promotes the art and hobby of window painting.** On colored acetate paper have outlines printed for painting pictures by numbers. These acetate sheets are stuck to one side of a window and anyone can paint a picture on the other side of the glass.

573. **Begin a business which produces framed reprints of interesting old patents**. Sell by post to professional people or have them stocked at gift shops or in an office.

574. **Start a comprehensive garden maintenance service**. Discuss with clients what work needs to be done to their gardens on a regular basis. People who use your service can have a beautiful garden and not do a minute of work in it themselves.

575. **Produce a series of music and sound effects audio CD's or MP3's** which are specially designed to aid the growth of household plants. For example, sounds might include the wind blowing and birds singing. Advertise in gardening and householders magazines.

576. **Research a Road or Highway**. Pick a well-known old and long road. Research and write the history of that road. Have a few hundred booklets printed and sell to the residents and businesses along the road. Route 66 for example has a great and storied history.

577. **Bargain Hunter**. If you love a bargain and know how to use coupons, specials, and unadvertised deals to make your penny-pinching go further, then you could help others learn **how to save money**—and turn a profit. Before you buy anything, you should visit **TheKrazyCouponLady.com.** She'll help you to help others become a frugal shopper on a mission. She's done amazingly well and is world renown. Now it's your turn to save and teach others.

578. **Enterprising Success Coach.** Create a course or write and publish a book about how to be more enterprising. Sell by placing ads in national newspapers. Have ad headlines like: 'Are you an enterprising person?', and 'Improve your life by being more enterprising'.

**579. Bring out a selection of pretty, non-picture postcards** which are specially designed for friends to send brief notes to each other. Have them stocked at stationers, newsagents and shops which sell greeting cards.

**580. Top Quality Soil.** Find a source of high-quality soil, package and sell through hardware stores and garden centers. Brand it, private label it and make it a staple for discriminating homeowners.

**581. Create a stop smoking club.** Hold club meetings at hired halls in various areas on different nights of the week. Employ a variety of techniques to help people to give up smoking. A great many people will be driven by the collective inspiration of the group.

**582. Have T-shirts printed with sci-fi messages on the front such as 'Alpha Centauri University'**, Visit Ancient Egypt with TWA's Time Travel Tours', 'Test fly a Centauri flying saucer, visit your local dealer', etc. Sell at sci-fi conventions and through sci-fi shops. Develop your own sales platform through Etsy.com or Shopify.com. Use POD (Print on demand) suppliers to print your shirts one at a time.

**583. Develop a range of Jewelry for ears.** Some of these Jewelry selections will not hang from earlobes like regular earrings, but gently clips to the top of the ears.

This Jewelry looks as if it if it is perched on top of the ears. A piece of ear top Jewelry might follow the curvature of each ear.

**584. Start a business which makes a range of quality old-fashioned long johns**. Produce a catalog and start a mail or online business. Especially popular in cold regions of the country.

**585. Consider taking up the career of a chiropody**. A chiropodist or podiatrist is a specialized foot doctor who treats people suffering from lower limb or common foot problems such as bunions and ingrown toenails. Send for a prospectus from a school of chiropody. Take a course and, after graduation, open your own practice. Licensing in some states may be required. Another name could be Nail Technologist.

**586. Start a computerized horse-racing results prediction service.** There are many systems available for selecting a winning horse. Base your computer program on any or a mixture of these systems. Send forecasts on a regular basis to subscribers.

**587. Be a travelling manicurist**. Build up a regular round of clients at offices and private residences. Send a leaflet about your service to businesses and private residences and advertise in the local papers, and on social media.

588. **Publish a monthly newsletter which gives inspiration to those trying to lose weight.** Successful dieting often depends on what's going on in a person's mind. A newsletter such as this can help to prepare a person, with various stories of success from those who have succeeded in losing weight and a selection of techniques to make the process easier. Write your book after your many student success stories.

589. **Start a mail or online business which sells stop smoking aids.** For example: dummy cigarettes, advice booklets, herbal aids, inspirational CD's or MP3's, charts and posters. You can produce many of these products yourself and buy the others from wholesalers. Write a definitive book on How to Stop Smoking and publish in bookstores and online.

590. **Inventor.** Begin a service which sells the reproduction rights to formulae for making products such as stain removers, special glues and toilet water. Your audience will come from business opportunity seekers who want to reproduce these formulae for reselling and housewives and cleaning services. You can also sell the formulae as 'household secrets' through classified ads in women's magazines and online.

591. **Medical Transcribers**. Workers take audio recordings made by doctors and other health care professionals and transcribe them into readable reports. Given the complexity of the language and the critical need for accuracy, specialized training is helpful. But many employers are glad to offer on-the-job training, according to the U.S. Bureau of Labor Statistics, or BLS. And, the job conditions can be cushy: Most are in comfortable office settings, and telecommuting is common. The pay averages $17.86 per hour for transcribers at medical and diagnostic laboratories, and you may be able to wedge in the work during evenings and weekends.

592. **Losing Weight Consultant**. Create an audio CD/MP3 or DVD course about how to lose weight. This might employ techniques of self- hypnosis or subliminal suggestion and combine fat-burning exercises and best ways to burn calories. PX90 and Tae Bo were very successful programs and sold hundreds of thousands of copies. Sell from ads in slimming and women's magazines. Create your own testimonial website too of your student's success stories.

593. **Create a Premium First Aid and Safety Kit For Your Car**. Create your premium roadside car kit that can be placed in your trunk until you need it.

From reflective roadside triangles, to flares to flat-tire sealant cans, to blanket, one to two days of food, water, etc. Sell Charge $75-$100 for your kit and make it the best on the market. Sell through your own website.

594. **Dog walking business.** Starting a dog walking business is becoming really mainstream these days. If you love dogs, love the outdoors and really like walking (75% of the job) then this could be for you. The average dog-walker makes $13.72 an hour but that rate goes up with experience. Payscale.com.

595. **Open a school of massage.** Learn all that you can about every kind of massage possible and get certified in each massage technique. Teach, or organize the teaching of, massage to those interested in becoming professionals. Depending on your certifications, proximity to metropolitan areas, etc., you should be able to charge $6-$15,000 per student and have a long list of those desiring to learn your techniques and business building practices.

596. **Company Food/Products Broker**. If you have a gift for speaking, can make a fantastic one-on-one presentation and are diligent in following-through with projects and people, you should find amazing food and hardline products in your region and offer to represent their products to major retailers and buyers.

Take a 2-5% commission on all sales to stores you get into. Take orders from the retail buyers and convey them to your manufacturer. Keep track of orders and commissions. Bill the manufacturer on terms and get paid. Do this over and over again and represent dozens of companies to retailers. Ask retailers what they are looking for, and then go and source it out. You can make a great six-figure living doing this and its fun.

597. **Reproduce old black and white or sepia,** a reddish-brown color associated particularly with monochrome photographs of a town as postcards, posters and framed prints. Have them stocked in a wide variety of local shops.

598. **Produce biographical photographs of celebrities.** For example, read all about the Beatles or the Rolling Stones to discover; their places of birth, schools, first places of work, houses they once lived in, etc. Take photographs of these places, and put dates of birth below portrait photographs and sell to fans.

599. **Pizza Delivery.** Pizza delivery drivers need a car, are willing to work dinner hours and weekends when customers order pizza. Decent hourly wage and tips for deliveries can be a great PT job.

600. **International Marketing and Law.** As the emphasis on global business and trade grows, organizations will be

looking for individuals who will have the education, experience, and skill set to navigate areas like international marketing, law, tax codes, work and environmental regulations, and even morals and ethics. Individuals who want to take advantage of this trend will likely need a law degree with an emphasis on international law or an international MBA. Excellent communication skills, as well as knowledge and/or fluency in one or more languages will also help. Individuals who follow this path should also be willing to live in several different countries over the course of their careers, as this will be a future trend.

601. **Design and produce a range of amusing self-adhesive stickers for children**. The stickers might feature jokes, funny faces and streetwise statements. Distribute to wholesalers, newsagents and toyshops.

602. **Become a Virtual Assistant.** Organized, detail-oriented people with strong computer and communication skills are often great candidates for virtual assistant positions. Over the course of this work, you may be called upon to make hotel reservations, set up appointments and meetings, type letters and buy supplies. While a typical administrative assistant may perform these same tasks from an office setting, a virtual assistant can work on projects from home. Outside of normal business hours, virtual assistants can do work that isn't time-sensitive, including internet research, data entry,

accounting and invoicing. Starting wage in most cities is $16 to $20/hour.

603. **Run Errands and Do Cleaning**. These jobs won't be a big asset on your resume, but they can be a great way to earn extra cash. Here are a few sites to choose from: **www.JobRunners.com** offers home cleaning, delivery, admin support, and handyman work to the public. **www.Handy.com** offers services focused on home cleaners and handymen. **www.TaskRabbit.com** which offers everything from moving to event and party planning.

604. **Jazz Recordings Broker.** Start a mail or online business which sells new and second-hand Jazz records. Many rare and classic Jazz recordings are released in the US regularly and it's making a great comeback with new aficionados. Sell your Jazz recordings on your website.

605. **Begin a stamp club which sends philatelists a set of stamps every month**. The sets might be either, thematic or newly issued by a country chosen by the collector. Charge a fee for each month's collector series.

606. **Child and Senior Care worker**. Websites like **SitterCity,com** and **UrbanSitter.com** make it easy to find nanny and babysitting opportunities near you. You can also try posting a message on **NextDoor.com** or Craigslist to offer your babysitting services to local families. **Care.com** is

perfect if you want to work with adults and the senior care market. The ability to control your work hours and the relatively high pay make these jobs ideal for college students and retired people.

607. **Employ homeworkers to make knitwear products**. Go the buyers of retailers or small shop owners to provide your knitwear.

608. **Pet Care.** We all love our pets. Animal lovers rejoice: now you can get paid to spend time with your furry friends. Dog-sitting websites like **www.DogVacay.com** and **www.Rover.com** offer boarding, cleaning, walking, day care, and more for doggies. If you're interested in caring for cats, **www.Holidog.com** offers services for both dogs, cats and birds. This is well suited for people with limited, inconsistent schedules who need to earn a small amount of extra cash. Visit their websites and get registered. This could be the start of a whole new chapter in your life.

609. **Become an importer and distributor of car accessories** (or anything you desire). Conduct thorough research in countries throughout the world to find car accessories not readily available here. Check out **www.AliExpress.com** for unique ideas at wholesale pricing. Always look for the best and most reputable suppliers when doing any importing. Check reputations from the comments that are made about these manufacturer too. This will give you

a good snapshot at how well these companies manage their business. Focus on companies with 3+Stars and up with multiple shipping options and fast deliveries to your market.

610. **Natural History Repository**. Begin a mail or online business which sells books and study equipment to those interested in natural history.

611. **Anniversary Reminder Service.** Start a company which organizes business anniversary celebrations. Devise celebration packages and sell to businesses who have been in business for 1, 5, 10, 20, 21, 25, 50, 60, 75, or 100 years. Locate potential clients by searching records to discover when firms were formed. Expand this to personal anniversary reminder services for those who always seem to wait to the last minute to remember that special anniversary.

612. **Send-Out-Card Business**. Every business can benefit by sending out timely greeting cards to their clients and business associates. Send-Out-Cards does it all, automatically for about a dollar a card, personally printed too. Never forget another important birthday, anniversary or special date again. By lining up businesses and individuals, you can have a very strong monthly business. Startup is inexpensive. Upside is high.

613. **Start a modern art rental business.** Rent out everything from metal sculptures to mobile art. Your potential clients will include all image conscious businesses with reception areas, courtyards offices or forecourts.

614. **Women's Birthday Planner.** Begin a business which organizes and specializes in adventure holidays for women. The holidays should be designed to help women develop their skills and abilities related to: management, persuasiveness, problem solving, leadership, creative thinking, etc.

615. **Start a central membership agency for joining fan clubs.** Persuade established fan clubs to become part of your program. Recruit people by advertising in numerous pop and rock publications, Facebook etc. You take a commission on all membership fees. Check out **www.AliExpress.com** for unique ideas too.

616. **History Book Sales.** Set up a mail or online company which sells local history books. Put together a selection of local history books for most cities and towns in the country. Produce a catalog and sell through media advertising and Craigslist.

617. **Start a Mary Kay or Avon business.** Call on clients once every six to eight weeks to sell cosmetics.

The cosmetics should have a special features, for example, perhaps the cosmetic do not involve cruelty to animals, or are based on herbs or are mineral based. Offer makeovers and build repeat business client's list. Mary Kay and Avon are two of the largest and most trusted cosmetic companies in the world. Find out about their commission programs and working for them to see if you enjoy it before going fulltime.

**618. Design and manufacture kits for making unusual furniture.** For example: tables that hang from the ceiling, chairs with odd shapes, stylistic plant stands, etc. Produce a catalog about your product and start a mail or online business. Get creative here.

**619. Employment Consultant.** Start an online blog on how to get a better job. Provide subscribers with advice on where to look, completing application forms quickly and easily, interview techniques, interview preparation, etc. The competitive nature of the job market means that the extra advice provided by your blog could make all the difference in the world to a job applicant's success. Develop a book series that covers these areas in depth and sell on Amazon and CreateSpace.

**620. Chocolate and Candy Maker.** Begin your candy and chocolate making journey selling your confections, sweets and hand-made chocolates at county fairs, flea markets, and community events.

Get proper business and food handling licensing and begin selling boxes of your newly branded chocolates to companies, weddings, and through party plans and fund-raising groups. Buy your stock from small producers of confectionery or create your own. Be the candy lady everyone loves and the one everyone must visit.

621. **Home sharing is hot right now**. Got an extra room in your home or apartment? Websites like **www.Homestay.com**, **www.Airbnb.com**, and **www.FlipKey.com** allow you to rent out your home or room to vacationers and travellers. Put your room on the availability list during holidays like Thanksgiving or Christmas break, when demand (and rates) are highest and see what happens. This is a great way to earn cash without having to spend time at a second job. Note: imagine having multiple rooms or cabins in areas that visitors want to visit? This industry is threatening the hotel and hospitality industry in a big way.

622. **Buy a selection of local history books, pamphlets, posters and postcards** from the publishers at trade prices. Earn from selling these via website in your area. Promote locally or regionally. Sell to libraries around the country. If you'd like to sell to US libraries, who buy $28 billion dollars a year in books, check this out. **https://bit.ly/1xWbqDC.**

623. **Design and make a selection of patchwork hats, caps, jackets, dresses**, etc. Find retailers who will stock your products. Or design and produce kits so that anyone can make their own patchwork products. Place classified ads in needlework magazines and sell by mail.

624. **Become a delivery driver**. You can also become a delivery driver for a local restaurant or find driving positions through **www.Grubhub.com, www.Sprig.com, www.Postmates.com, www.Doordash.com**,. The list goes on. Good pay...solid work too.

625. **Publish an audio CD/MP3 of spicy jokes.** Sell through gift shops, resorts and malls. The hope is that holiday-makers might send a saucy CD/MP3 home instead of a spicy postcard. With each CD/MP3 include a small card for writing a gift message.

626. **Organize the production of business greeting cards**. Ever notice the lack of business related thank you for your business cards, glad to have you as our new client cards, etc. in the market today? Design the cards for a particular selection of businesses, for example, medical doctor, chiropractic and legal services where the owner of those practices can send welcoming cards to their new clients. The cards should have pictures relevant to the chosen business. Sell by direct mail or through your online website targeting professionals.

**627. Set up a health food catering service.** Do the catering at a wide range of occasions such as private parties, business functions and luncheons for staff, weddings, etc. Advertise in health food shop noticeboards and send copies of your menu to businesses along with pricing. Offer special pricing for first time clients.

**628. Freelance Salesperson or Manufacturer's Rep.** Earn an income from being a freelance salesperson. Place ads in business or trade publications which reads 'Freelance Salesperson/ Manufacturer's Rep. Available. Anything Considered. Contact...' Don't accept the first offer, but consider each one and accept the one you find the most suitable. Work on a commission basis or accept an in-house position with a company willing to pay you well.

**629. Cafeteria Worker.** Before you say not me, working in a high school, elementary or university dining cafeteria will require little to no experience and will have a higher pay than other restaurant jobs. It may not be the most glamorous of work, but it will earn you money and free meals, saving you a significant amount of food-prep time and money. As you become fulltime, health, dental and insurance benefits will pop in as well. Bon appetite!

630. **Motorcycle Memorabilia**. Begin an online business which sells a selection of products of particular interest to motorcycle enthusiasts. In your catalog include; badges, jackets, embroidery service, clothing, cult ornaments, etc. Advertise in motorcycle magazines, Craigslist, etc.

631. **Sell Ring, Simply Safe and other video security equipment** door-to-door that can be for businesses and/or homeowners. Put together a brochure to leave behind. TV commercials are driving this security trend right now too. This could be expanded by using commissioned sales personnel to sell for you. Get products at wholesale and sell retail. With security for homeowners and businesses a big priority, offer installation as well. Access to their homes and businesses can be by the use of their phones now. Find a wholesale source for the products and offer to install for a nominal fee.

632. **Child Care and Babysitting Business.** With husbands and wives working more outside of the home, having quality childcare you can count on is vital to every family with kids. Imagine watching up to six children at $100-$300/week per child?

633. **Buy Low and Sell High.** Buy and sell second hand household goods from local garage sales and flea markets and upsell them on your own website or at your yard sale.

634. **Electronics Repair Business.** If you're the sort of person who takes apart the computer for fun, opens up radios, rips into vacuum cleaners, or takes apart a television because you can, operating an electronics repair shop out of your home or garage is a natural business step for you. In particular, repairing iPads, phones and other e would electronics provide you with a great deal of business, as many tablet users are looking for a less expensive way to fix smashed screens and other damages that can be costly through the manufacturer. Open up your mind and do a little research on what areas of repair can bring you the best income. Median salary: $49,170 as of this publication date.

635. **Area Tour Guide**. Are you undeniably passionate about your college campus or small town or large city? Put it to good use as a paid tour guide. This will give you public speaking practice, exercise, and a chance to convince prospective travelers to move to your area or just enjoy the sights. This job is simple and fun as long as you are prepared to be conversationally sharing unique, unknown information for the entirety of the tour. Great money can be made too in short tours as well. $20-$30 per person for an hour. Children less perhaps.

**636. Start a school of psychic phenomena, ESP and the unknown**. Offer potential students easy-to-do courses on subjects such as UFO's, ESP, sea monsters, ghosts, etc. Advertise in a wide range of publications.

**637. If you live near a port or marina. Start and operate a boat and yacht valeting service**. Cleaning and maintaining boats and yachts can be very lucrative. But first seek expert advice from someone knowledgeable about boating or yachting and what is involved in marine valeting. **Here's a site** to check out if you're interested.

**638. Popcorn Machine**. Purchase a popcorn machine and sell at little league baseball games, flea markets, craft shows, sporting events like soccer or football games, church events, and anywhere a crowd gathers. Most of us can't resist the smell of freshly made popcorn. Popcorn markups are very high too.

**639. Create an EBay store online**. Sell everything from books, to crafts to wholesale items that you've purchased in bulk and sell it on EBay. Always important too, to see what your competition on EBay is selling a like tem for. Undercut a little to move your products faster. Customer feedback is crucial for your store's success, so always find ways to satisfy your customers.

While there are many very successful EBay shop owners throughout the world, don't put all of your sales in a single platform. Spread sales out over Etsy and Amazon too. Better yet, create your own sales site and build your customer list there. You have complete control over your site. You don't with the EBay, Etsy or Amazon. Always play be the rules. Take care of customers and get great feedback for your long term success. Now go list some items on EBay and get cracking.

640. **Do bottle art. Paint local scenery** and other artistic images on the exterior of tiny glass bottles. Sell as souvenirs or ornaments.

641. **Fax Lunch Menus to Local Businesses**. Lunch time for many is the one sure meal of the day. Faxing out your restaurant's menu and taking phone orders can be a real boost for a local eatery. Pizza, Mexican food, sub-shops, can all benefit with a special offer attached. Though there may be laws restricting the faxing to individuals, your being able to fax businesses is allowed in most areas. Offer to restaurants your service and fax to a thousand or so local corporations, and businesses their menu for a fee. Line-up 5-10 businesses and do this weekly or every other week for them. They'll gladly pay you to generate sales volume for them. Put together their successful fax ad too and they'll be with you for a while.

642. **Gold Prospecting**. Begin an online business which serves those interested in gold prospecting. Sell equipment, supplies and books. Also publish your own guide to digging for gold too. Many forms of gold mining include sluice boxes in rivers, gold panning, and staking gold claims and digging for precious metals. Some knowledge of the process and gold and silver itself is crucial for your success.

643. **Produce a series of booklets about how to buy and run various types of businesses**. Each booklet might cover a business such as a social media manager, real estate agent, running an Etsy or Shopify craft business online or an EBay store, etc. Place classified ads in newspapers and magazines which advertise shops for sale and sell your booklets online.

644. **Commission the drawing of political cartoons** which have an anti-establishment theme. Have these printed on postcards or posters and sell through shops popular with young adults.

645. **Herb Farming.** Gardening can be very relaxing, and potentially very lucrative. With both the increased interest in alternative therapies and the demand for locally grown and organic foods, an herb farmer can find plenty of customers, particularly if you're in an urban area.

While this does require some space for growing, herb farming can be done in a fairly small space and nearly any home can be slightly modified to allow for an extensive herb garden. Local health food stores and farmer's markets are good places to get started. Know how to price your herbs and costs that are involved as margins can be skinny in this business.

**646. Be a home-visiting pre-school teacher**. Your task is to prepare children for a successful start at school. Assignments can be made, reading can be taught and social skills learned as children prepare to be Kindergarteners.

**647. Buy a candy cotton floss making machine.** Sell your cotton candy at fairs, carnivals, garage sales, Little League games or from any site where there is a continuous flow of people who are enjoying their leisure and where children who love cotton candy are. Great markups too. Kids and dentists will love you.

**648. Design a range of blank achievement certificates** for use by sports clubs and schools. Have them printed and sell by direct mail. Make up some funny ones too. Sell as gag gifts from small shops.

**649. Hand paint nostalgic scenes and old advertisements on mirrors.** Use vinyl plastic cutting machines to print them. Sell through gift shops or from a table at local gift shows and flea markets.

650. **Produce T-shirts which are printed with the names of local schools**. Have them stocked at local retailers or other suitable shops close to each school.

651. **Design and make soft toys which are suitable for shelf ornaments**. For example: Alice in Wonderland characters mounted on stands which have a label giving the name of each character. The high quality of workmanship should allow you to charge prices to give you a good profit.

652. **Carve wooden ornaments**. Attach to one side of the ornament a sticky baked material or magnet. They can then be added to car dashboards or to fridges.

653. **Day Trading**. Put together a course about how to become a stock-market day trader. Learn all that you can about trends and companies that are on the move. Read all that you can from authorities in this area too. Paper trade until you are ready to jump into the market with real cash.

654. **Writing Good Fiction Dialog.** Bring out a correspondence course or audio CD/MP3 course, about how to write good dialogue for fiction. Fiction is the hottest genre at a bookstore or on Amazon today. Being able to create believable and credible dialog is crucial for this market. Sell through ads in publications for writers and have your own website that promotes your dialog book or CD/MP3.

**655. Brand Ambassador**. If you are friendly, energetic, outgoing, and self-motivated, your work as a brand ambassador for a local startup or business can be very rewarding. This position is great for those who want to gain experience in a number of special roles. You will likely be asked to do cold calling, email marketing, social media management, distributing flyers, and attending events and tradeshows to represent your company. Based on your performance, there can also be an opportunity to grow within the company.

**656. Stamp or coin collectors.** Start an international correspondence club for stamp or coin collectors. The benefits of membership would include being able to swap stamps, coins, magazines, books and information with other members. Match stamp and coin collectors according to their interests and produce a periodic publication for all members too.

**657. Make loveable pocket-sized soft toys and hang on a rack for display in shops**. Give the toys a catchy name like 'Pocket Pets'. Approach local drug and toy stores with your "I'm local" sales pitch.

**658. Home Staging Company**. Have you seen those wonderful HGTV shows that flip homes for a profit? They take run-down, beat up homes with lots of work to do on them, and then fix them up and sell them for a profit.

Well one the most important parts of that process is called Home staging is where potential home buyers see the home with furniture in it after rehabbing is done. Companies have a large inventory of modern furniture and home décor they can draw from. If rearranging furniture is your idea of fun, home staging is a great home-based business. You will help sellers get their homes looking beautiful so they sell as quickly as possible. Home Staging companies, in big cities, charge $3500-$4000 to stage a home for a month until the home sells. Well worth it and just part of the cost of selling the home faster at top dollar.

659. **Give private instruction about how to make money.** If you've got a flair for making money, it's time to share it. It might be about making money from business and investments, flipping homes, professional public speaking, or Cryptocurrency and forex trading. You might, for example, use some of the ideas listed in this selection as worthwhile money-makers. Prepare lesson plans on the subjects you wish to cover and teach a set course. Market anywhere. Everyone wants to make more money.

660. **Set up a business which organizes weight loss trips and holidays**. These holidays are not on health farms but consist of long distance walking, diet instruction, and discussion amongst participants.

A person who wants to lose weight goes on a one, two or four week holiday which would consist of walking and exercising for most of the day, following a strict diet and evenings of discussion groups. Can be very fun and rewarding too. Setup a website that explains the vacation program and take reservations and money from the site.

661. **Design and make a selection of lucky charm key-rings**. For example, make a key-ring fob which is a wooden or metal number seven or four-leaf clover. Mount them on a rack and have them stocked at suitable retailers. Sell at flea markets as well.

662. **Organize the production and sales of potted plants along roadsides or in your front yard.** These plants will appeal to renters and homeowners alike. A sign and a nicely grown potted plant is all you need to start. Flowers or vegetables can get you started.

663. **Sell a wide range of postcards and souvenirs** from a roadside stand or through local retailers. Get display racks to make it easier for customers to go through your selection.

664. **Graphic Designer.** Another up and coming position that has wide appeal is a graphic designer. If you have an excellent design eye and know how to use Adobe Photoshop and Illustrator, there are endless job possibilities for you. Work as a freelance designer, create content for local

businesses or find an internship at a local marketing agency. The pay range is wide depending on your experience, the company and the complexity of the job, but hours can be flexible and the work can be remote. Rewarding work too.

**665. Sell Sand Castle Making Kits at the Beach.** Build elaborate sand castles or sand sculptures at the seaside and accept donations from those who want to show appreciation of your work. Better yet, publish a "how-to" book with dozens of ideas on the subject. Sell it on Amazon or at the beach with all the supplies a beach-goer will need to impress their kids. Create a "tools pack" of plastic accessories to make sand sculptures and castles so much more fun. Your beach is your office.

**666. Begin a service as a car broker to help owners sell their cars**. An auto brokers helps retail customers find cars from other dealerships. The broker acts as an agent for their client. For the purpose of finding, negotiating and buying their car for a fee or commission. Why would a client want to pay a fee for this service? Time and money savings! Brokers know the price of vehicles and will get you the best price possible, while locating exactly what you want in your next car. Like a real estate broker, hiring a professional can make all the difference in the world. If you have this knowledge and the negotiating skills, you make this a very lucrative business with a little advertising and marketing.

667. **Start a fortune telling gift service for new born babies**. When a baby is born a fortune-teller provides a written statement about their future. Such a statement would make an ideal birth gift. Advertise in the classified columnist of a variety of publications.

668. **Become a Personal Organizer.** If you're someone who reorganizes closets for fun, and has mad personal organizing skills, you should offer up your services to harried and disorganized individuals and businesses. This position can easily work into a fulltime gig as an administrative assistant for a company professional who is just crazy busy too.

669. **Become an Astrologist**. By understanding the basic nature of planetary energies, and how those energies are expressed through different signs and in different houses or areas of life, the ASTROLOGER can pinpoint strengths and weaknesses, and can foresee how a person is likely to react to any particular situation. Provide private readings to clients and/or provide your services to an online astrology site or a group of newspapers in the form of a column.

670. **Set up a business which teaches foreign languages**. The courses might consist of both, audio CD's or MP3's for learning to speak and written material for learning to write the language.

671. **Bring out an online course about creative thinking** and attract students by advertising in national newspapers and magazines. The ads might have a headline like 'Do people say you lack imagination?', or 'The amount of money you make is limited only by your imagination'.

672. **Put together an audio CD/MP3 course about how to be a successful disc jockey.** Sell from ads in music publications and have it stocked in record shops.

673. **Produce a series of biographical audio CD's or MP3's about well-known businesspeople**. Bring out a catalog and send it to business and professional people. Or start a monthly club where a subscriber receives a different CD/MP3 every month.

674. **Take an ordinary magnifying glass, package it and call it 'The Gardener's Magnifying Glass'.** Package it with what to look for under a magnifying glass in your garden. Identify aphids, bugs and weeds that will destroy your garden. Distribute to hardware shops or sell by mail from ads in gardening magazines.

675. **Open a Crystal, Rock and Gemstone Store**. It's become very commonplace today. Healing crystals aren't a trend anymore, they're a movement. And what was once just

considered a "woo-woo" practice, previously relegated to hippies and covens, has now entered the daily conversation. Healing crystals and gemstones such as rose quartz and moldovite can likely be spotted on your colleague's desk and shamans are now part of people's roster of healing experts. Even celebrities are wearing their crystals loud and proud. Know your gemstones and you've got the beginning of a business that's on the upswing.

676. **Create A TeleMedical Business**. One of the hottest new businesses now is getting bigger. The Country's largest health care insurer is putting telemedicine on par with a regular trip to the doctor's office, effectively saying a video visit is as good as brick-and-mortar medicine. Imagine saying "ahhhh to the doctor via Skype or FaceTime for your strep throat and getting your antibiotic prescription sent to your local drugstore in a few minutes. United Healthcare has announced a partnership with three telemedicine companies to cover video-based doctor visits just as it covers in-person visits. The tech set has for decades predicted that we would one day get our medical care via video chat, but it wasn't until recently that forward-thinking physicians started taking the promise of telemedicine seriously. The decision by so influential a player in the healthcare industry, is saying to telemedicine that we believe that technology in the mainstream is viable. This may very be the next big thing in healthcare delivery.

677. **Organize holidays for people at American farms and ranches**. First advertise in the States for farmers and ranch owners who want to have paying guests. Then advertise in a variety of publications in this country for clients. Or, **Research, write and produce a manual or correspondence course about 'How to start your own holiday organizing business'.** This might cover everything from organizing walking holidays to conventional sightseeing holidays. Sell to opportunity seekers.

678. **Begin a mail or online business which sells things related to cult figures** such as Nikola Tesla, L. Ron Hubbard, Leonardo Da Vinci, John Lennon, James Dean, Elvis, Marilyn Monroe, etc. Sell things such as press cuttings, photographs, audio CD's or MP3's, books, etc.

679. **Design and manufacture face painting kits.** In each kit have a spectrum of colors and a selection of designs which can be easily copied. Take your skill to fairs, local fund-raising events, concerts etc., and charge for your work. Have great designs for children and adults alike. Get your kits stocked at shops which sell toys, novelties or artist's materials.

680. **Produce an audio CD/MP3 course about positive thinking.** Change your state and you can change your life. Learn about vibration and various binaural beats to change your state of mind. Coach your customers. Sell by direct mail and online.

681. **Dog trainer**. If you love dogs, and love to see a happy and obedient animal, maybe being a dog trainer The average pay for a Dog Trainer job in the US is $39,500 a year. **ZipRecruiter.com** scanned its database of millions of jobs in order to estimate the most accurate salary range for Dog Trainer jobs in the United States. The average annual salary in California is $39,000, which is -$500 lower than the national average of $39,500. The average Dog Trainer salary in Modesto, CA is $39,000.

682. **Produce a library of audio CD's or MP3's about "How to Sing like an American Idol."** Sell by direct mail or your website. Have them stocked in bookshops and music stores too.

683. **At tourist sites take photographs** of holiday makers with a man dressed as a gorilla, or other amusing costume.

684. **Make Owl Boxes.** Every farmer, nut grower, vineyards, orange and lemon farmer need owl boxes so that owls will have a place to live. Boxes are placed at elevations of 6-30 feet, depending on the owl species you're attracting. They will kill rodents, rats, field mice and small animals. Barn owls for example eat about 6 small rodents (mice) every night or 2200 rodents a year. Owls will save farmers thousands of dollars in lost fruit and pesticides too. Owl boxes retail for $120 to $250 not including the pole.

**685. Design and produce a series of wall charts for children.** One chart might ask a child to record one good deed a day; another might ask a child to record new words learnt; a third might be for recording the weather or what happened at school.

**686. Start an online catalog which specializes in products which aid in abstinence**. For example, products for giving up: Smoking, Swearing, Nail Biting, Drinking, etc.

**687. Set up a school of variety entertainment**. Teach students about the variety entertainment business, how to emcee an event, proper word usage, introductions etc. Also show beginners how to improve any acts of their own which they would like to perform.

**688. Business Broker**. Help small business owners sell their businesses. Many owners will simply close their doors when perhaps they could sell it with some encouragement from you. You'll estimate the value of the business with inventory, good will in the community, accounts receivable, etc. and then advertise the price of the business in business selling publications. You as the broker can make money several ways. One is to take a 10% commission on the sale or transfer of the business, or another is to simply buy the business at a discount yourself if it looks promising, and then install good management in it, clean it up and operate it as a new business.

689. **Use pastels or charcoals to do original pictures** of tourist sites. Sell, framed or unframed, as quality souvenirs.

690. **Design garden ornaments.** Ornaments create a special effect on summer days. Made from glass, mirrors, and lighted from solar cells. Start your business which builds and sells your designs. You might advertise in local publications, online at sites like Craigslist or EBay, or sell directly you one of a kind creations at your local stores or craft fairs.

691. **Begin a book of the month club for those who want to learn the principles of management or sales management.** Each book takes the form of an instruction manual on parts of the sales and closing process. These books are strung together to make a complete sales and or management course.

692. **Use leather to make key-ring fobs.** Burn designs or put studs into the fobs and add a key-ring. Sell from a fair, craft show or a local retail outlet.

693. **Design and produce a selection of amusing bumper stickers.** For example: 'Keep your distance, or we might meet by accident', or 'Keep car mechanics poor, keep your distance'. Have them stocked at car accessory shops and service stations. Bumper stickers can be a complete business with display racks and a variety of messages. Brand yours for repeat sales.

**694. Put together a Christmas-In-A-Box decoration Pack.** In each pack include all the decorations needed to completely decorate a room of an average home. The packaging might include a picture of a room which shows where each of the decorations might go.

**695. Assertiveness Training.** Bring out an audio CD/MP3 course about how to be assertive at home and at work. How to ask for a raise at work etc. Use direct mail to sell the course to businesspeople, women and opportunity seekers.

**696. There's a strong need today for a Social Media Manager** in every small business and large one too. Think you've been wasting your time on FaceBook, Snapchat and Instagram? You've actually been gaining useful skills. Put those skills to good use by running the social media accounts for a local business or startup. Some of these positions can also be done remotely, which is great for the busy college student or mom with small children at home.

**697. Chess and Board Games.** Create a selection of products related to chess and board games. For example: books, ornaments, framed prints, chess (or game) playing accessories, etc. Produce a catalog and sell by mail or from your online website

698. **Design and make a selection of baby christening and blessing outfits**. Sell the outfits by mail or online or through shops which sell children's clothing.  Also sell from your online presence too.

699. Set up a booth in a tourist town which **sells all kinds of belts, jewelry, crystals, aromatherapy oils, from the highly fashionable to the personalized.** Brand your selections. Advertise in local tourist publications given away at the local Chamber of Commerce and promote and online everywhere.

700. **Kite Manufacturing**. Make kites which feature Stars and Stripes or the colors of popular football teams. Package and have stocked at suitable retailers. Sell at beaches, parks and anywhere people gather for outdoor events.

701. **Open a website which sells hats and other headgear.** Your stock will include: ladies hats, scarves, men's caps. Have the capability to personalize then and see greater interest.

702. **Start a company which designs and manufactures notice boards or business card boards for the home and office.** These might have a special feature, for example, cover the boards with a fabric which has an exotic design or make boards which have an unusual shape.

For offices or businesses, develop a nice business card display board. Local businesses will pay you $10-$15 a month to have their cards displayed in your business. With a 30 card display at $10 a month, retailers gross $3600 per year. You sell the board for $125-$150 each.

703. **Produce a course about how to design saleable vinyl stickers for all sorts of projects.** The main market for this would be people who want to create a vinyl sticker business and display their works on EBay, Etsy, in Facebook forums or on Craigslist.

704. **Take everyday objects such as clocks, watches, computers and calculators. Remove the outer casing and mount them** to make educational aids or ornaments. Also you might label the most important parts of each object.

705. **Recreate classic chess games on video.** Start a business which hires and sells these to chess enthusiasts. Smaller market but loyal followers of the chess masters is your target group.

706. **Start a miniature brassware decorations of the month club**. If you like to work with various metals, have a real skill in brass work, welding and brazing, this might be for you. Produce an online catalog on your website and promote it on free sites.

707. **Create a course about how to compose and write musical hymns**. Advertise in the religious press and church bulletins.

708. **Produce an encyclopedia of self-improvement on audio CD's or MP3's.** This should cover all subjects related to self-improvement and might be 20-50 CD's or MP3's in length. Sell in monthly installments or as a complete course.

709. **Become a ghostwriter.** Everyone has a "book in them" but not everyone knows how to write a book. Help them. If you have a way with words, and really want to make a difference in someone's like, help them write their autobiography, or family history or help them research and write a non-fiction "how-to" help book. Depending on the number of words you write, interview time with them, and time you spend researching the content for the book, you can make $1000-$2,000 a book or more. You'll need a great computer and dictation software that will make it a breeze. Offer editing services after words too.

710. **Start a service which finds companions for those who want to go on cycling or hiking holidays or play tennis.** Advertise in publications for cyclists, hikers or tennis publications or on Craigslist.

711. **Take suitable sea-shells and sell them as sleep shells.** Those who have difficulty in sleeping at night listen to a sleep shell. The soothing sound of the sea will aid sleep.

712. **Organize overseas information gathering tours for businesspeople**. These might be for those who want to look at an overseas market or who want to visit similar businesses to their own in other countries. For example, consultants in this country can visit their foreign counterparts.

713. **Create a mail or online business which sells matchboxes and labels to collectors.** Collectors automatically receive the latest matchboxes each month. Alternatively you might put together a catalog of old and rare matchboxes.

714. **Do your own research to discover ghost stories from your region**. Record the best stories on audiotape. Have the CD's or MP3's duplicated and labelled and distribute to shops throughout the region covered.

715. **Frame photographs of well-known boxers**. Get these stocked at sports shops or sell by mail or online from ads in boxing and sports papers and magazines. Become the local framing expert for family and wedding portraits as well.

716. **Take and Get Paid For Surveys.** If you are looking for quick extra cash then signing up for sites like **MySurvey.com**, or **SurveyScout.com** can get you a nice side income with immediate results. You will not get rich doing surveys, but each site could net you anywhere from $30 to $300 per month. Some other popular survey sites include:

**InboxDollars.com, GlobalTestMarket.com, Harris PollOnline.com, EarningStation.com**

717. **Retail Cashier.** The cashier position is great because it requires little to no experience, offers flexible hours (depending on the place), and is readily available in most towns. Don't be fooled by the title: you'll likely do some food prep and/or stocking shelves as well. You can take this skill to any city or country in the world as customer service is the key to respectable cashiering. Learn to make change easily too.

718. **Set up a quiz games club**. Club members compete against each other to win quizzes through an online game site. The quizzes could be published in on your site which would also give the answers to the previous quizzes.

719. **Invent and make wooden 2-D and 3-D executive puzzles.** For example: 3-D puzzles which have lots of interlocking pieces. Have them stocked at gift shops and stationers.

720. **Make cotton gloves especially designed for coin collectors.** The gloves prevent the grease and moisture from fingers getting onto coins. Package the gloves and sell them from ads in coin collecting magazines or distribute to shops which sell collectible coins.

**721. Design and have printed novelty joke licenses**. Each license has a space for a name to be added. The license may state that the named person is: a genius, certified insane, backseat driver's license, international sex maniac, etc. Distribute to shops which sell souvenirs, jokes and gifts.

**722. Produce photographic business cards** and sell these direct to businesspeople. You might also produce blank photographic business cards for printers. For example a card features a photograph which is representative of a trade, a printer would print personal details next to the picture.

**723. Introduce to your region a service which mounts maps for businesses**. Keep a stock of local, national and international maps. Mount these maps in a professional manner to suit the wall space available at offices. Send out emails about your services to office managers.

**724. Open a bakery.** From your morning coffee to your kid's birthday cake, neighborhood bakeries can fill a vast number of small-town needs. Though owning and operating a bakery is hard work, if it's your life-long dream to produce pastries for the masses, it's a business idea that can be incredibly rewarding. Employing youth from your town is also a great way to give back and stay connected to your community. If you're a newbie to owning a business in a small town, doing research on opening a successful bakery is extremely important. You'll also want to familiarize yourself with how to price baked goods. Pretty soon, if you've satisfied the needs of your community, you could be "rolling in dough!" Sorry.

725. **Run for Political Office**. If you have a desire to serve your community (at a city council, mayor, county supervisor, congressperson, or state office) there is real money to be made. Many candidates begin by winning in non-paid offices like school boards and move up as their desire to seek higher offices increases. All the benefits (and headaches) are associated with running as a candidate and winning office. One thing that is vitally important though, is to have "core values" on what you truly believe and do your best top convey that belief to your constituency and how it will help them in the long run. If you are political in nature and love to serve others, consider running for office. Check out this great story of four candidates who ran for political office. **https://slate.me/2jilesj**. Very Inspiring.

726. **Become a Barista**. Although most of these jobs require some barista experience and training, they are a wonderful option for college students and those who desire to work for companies like Starbucks. Cafes are everywhere now, so you will meet hundreds of anxious coffee drinkers every day. Be prepared for some very early or late shifts too, as many cafes cater to the needs of their local community. Can be a nice position with advancement opportunities too.

727. **Design souvenir badges** which read 'I've been to (name of town)' or 'I love ...' Pay to have your badges professionally made. Arrange for shops in the named town to stock these badges.

728. **Each month produce an interesting lecture on audio CD/MP3**. Sell these through a monthly club. The subjects should be something which appeals to an established market such as science fiction fans, business opportunity seekers or sales people.

729. **Start a private school for florists.** Provide courses for those who want to either set up in business or want to get a job as a florist. Advertise in women's magazines. Charge tuition for their certification.

730. **Electronics, Drones and Phone dealer**. If you're looking to do something a little bit off the beaten path, now's the time. How about trying your hand as an electronics dealer specializing in drones and drone accessories? If this sounds a little too off the straight and narrow, trust us, it's worth a try. The commercial drone market is predicted to grow to over **$1 billion by 2022** according to **Grandviewresearch.com.** That's a massive market and you have the opportunity to get in early and be a disruptor. But go more mainstream with used computers and cell phones too can make a significant income for you and create tons of traffic for your store. Looking for an out-of-the-box small town business idea that everyone would love to visit? This is it!

731. **Design and organize the production of stop smoking penalty boxes.** Every time a person smokes, he or she pays a fine. Pay a plastics injecting moldings firm to manufacture the boxes. Distribute the finished plastic boxes to wholesalers and a wide range of retailers.

732. **Make good, old-fashioned wooden tool carriers** and have them stocked at hardware shops and tool shops. Or produce kits for making tool carriers and sell by mail or online from ads in DIY magazines. Every man and woman needs one of these for the garage or for the trunk of their car. This can go many different ways for those handy with wood and saws.

733. **Own an Ice Cream Shop with Candy.** Every town needs at least one right? Opening an ice cream/candy shop in a small town is a business idea guaranteed to draw a crowd. Knowing your product, being familiar with the most popular ice cream flavors, and having a willingness to work nights and weekends and around community events are all important factors to take into account. Just remember, this business comes with the challenges of seasonality. So, as we recommended boutique fitness businesses as great for cold weather climates, we are recommending ice cream/candy shops for areas that are warmer for more consistent year round sales. Find the perfect town with the perfect weather and this small town business idea is a no-brainer. Doesn't an ice cream sound good about now? And throw in some those candy thingies too.

734. **Make leather folders for salespeople to use when making presentations.** Have these stocked a stationers or produce a catalog about your range of folders and send it to businesses. Leather always says quality and reliability right?

735. **Sell holly and mistletoe door-to-door** during the Christmas period, Mistletoe is free everywhere. The baggies and printed labels can be done inexpensively. Mistletoe sells at Christmas time for $2.00 each or 3 for $5.00.

Everyone is always looking for a reason to kiss the ones they love. Let's give it to them shall we? This is a great way for children and teens to make money for Christmas gifts too.

**736. Movie Directing and Producing.** Put together a home study course about theatrical and movie directing and producing. Call this business your drama school. Use your video software, computer, lighting, video camera and phone to edit, be the basis of your Drama School. Create a YouTube channel to chart your progress as well, and use it to recruit new students. Monetize your YouTube channel as well. Students will include: amateur drama directors, professional actors and other theatre enthusiasts.

**737. Winning Coaching book.** Write and publish your book on winning in team sports. How to start and organize your own winning football or baseball teams. Sell from ads in sports magazines and Craigslist.

**738. Set up a window cleaning business.** Employ students and other young people to do the work. Build up lots of individual routes and employ a person for each one. Lock down a whole town or city as the "go-to" window washing firm in town.

739. **House Cleaning After Move-outs Business**. Place classified ads in newspapers and Craigslist which read: "Will thoroughly clean up houses after tenants move out." Call me. 555-555-1212. Work guaranteed. Approach property development companies, realtors and brokers and investors that need homes cleaned up quick. Typically, you dispose of everything in the home. You keep what's left in the homes too, like furniture and appliances, clothing and tools. Set your pricing based on the work and cleanup.

740. **Start a romantic time-capsule burying service.** A man or woman can immortalize the one they love by having a time-capsule buried to tell future generations about their loved one.

741. **Organize weekend retreats where individuals can have their career assessed by professional career advisers.** Advice should also be given on how to develop a career or how to make a change. Advertise in up-market or business publications. Be a Life or Career Coach. Easy certification.

742. **Write a career guide to self-employment**. Sell this through as many bookshops as possible and on Amazon and Barnes & Noble. Perhaps your guide will become an annual publication which will appeal to a new crop of people every year with new jobs and opportunities available too.

743. **Make life-size string puppets**. Each marionette puppet is controlled by someone standing on a roof, balcony or scaffold. Use for promotion or entertainment events, plays in the park and children's parties.

744. **Promotional Products Rep.** Begin am in-person or online firm which sells personalized, promotional items such as pens, towels, handkerchiefs, shirts, caps, notepads, combs, etc. Be a rep for a promotional company that already has put together the catalog. Advertise in up-market publications and visit local businesses who may have interest.

745. **Run a business which deals in the memorabilia of a region.** You can buy your stock from various sources, for example, history books from publishers, photographs from photo libraries and films and videos from film making and film distribution companies. Even from local college's sports team jerseys, helmets, balls etc.

746. **Write and publish an online blog which is specifically for budding and practicing freelance writers**. Give the newsletter a title like: 'Freelance Writer'. Give ideas and tips about how to sell their work and have a section for articles, letters and classified ads. Monetize your blog too.

**747. Become a wholesaler of spoken word audio CD's or MP3's.** You act as the middleman between publishers and retailers. This is still a growth area and it might not be long before every bookshop has many shelves of audio CD's, and DVD's. Do Voice-over work also if you have a unique, high quality voice.

**748. Set up a mail or online business which sells plans, equipment and supplies for making mosaics.** Also stained glass murals and art pieces. Produce a catalog and advertise in craft magazines.

**749. Sell cheap labor saving devices** door-to-door, for example: potato peelers, chip cutting machines, easy-to-use can openers, etc. Look at import sites like Alibaba.com and the bulk site at ebay.com.

**750. Design and make original fashion clothes**. Begin by selling your work from a craft table. This will give you the valuable experience of meeting your customers face-to-face. If you discover you can make clothes which are popular, branch out and sell to boutiques and online. Expand by hiring piece workers.

**751. Learn how to build garden fences and raised "grow boxes"** then start your own business.

Advertise your garden building business in local newspapers and offer to provide a free written estimate, building and installations too. Gardening is much more fun when you're standing instead of kneeling.

752. **Library Assistant.** Library jobs are one of the most convenient jobs to have as a student because of their relatively high pay and on-campus location. This position will give you plenty of customer service practice and the chance to interact with college students for most of your shift. Best of all, there is usually plenty of time to do your homework. If you're in a public library position, a library assistant is equally enjoyable work, full-time or part-time.

753. **Design, make and distribute souvenir pottery doorstops**. These might be imprinted with the name of a resort or a view of tourist scenery.

754. **Visit offices during lunch breaks, or before work begins, to give "keep-fit classes."** Line up a regular monthly business route for lunchtimes with several companies.

755. **Produce a selection of political and moral T-shirts**. These will be designs to publicly express a person's opinion. Sell at demonstrations and through ads in the political press. Create a mail or online catalog.

756. **Begin a business which organizes short courses and seminars for salespeople**. A guest successful sales personality might be selected to give each lesson. The subjects you cover might include: "Closing More Sales," 'How to Double Your Sales' and 'How to Beat Your Competitors'. See what people like Grant Cardone have done in this sales arena.

757. **Start a business which records interviews with celebrities.** Market these podcasts on audio CD's or DVD's just as if you were selling books or DVD's. Sell these from your online store and from your own online catalog. Open a podcast also and a YouTube channel and begin to monetize it with advertising and views. For the CD's/DVDs, try to get them stocked in book and music stores and local libraries too.

758. **Arrange for greeting messages to be carved into stone.** Imagine a large stone at your business's entry way that says, for example, "We want raving fans" or "Our Guarantee is written in Stone". Start by selling your services to small local businesses who are looking for distinctive ways to insure their customers a successful buying experience. Have a tombstone engraving company do the engraving on a great piece of stone (not a head stone) and then take the difference that you charge the retailer. Show ideas to business owner around your state.

**759. Jump start your career as a freelance journalist**. If you have a way with words and love to write, then Newspapers, magazines, radio and TV shows are always interested in success stories and local news that matters and would like to talk with you. Perhaps start with finding and writing about people from humble backgrounds who have been successful in their life's endeavors. The best way to find such people is to advertise for them and ask around to folks you know. Approach editors too for stories they'd like to see written. Deliver your story on-time to the editor and see how that works for your longterm career.

**760. Cut divining rods (from willow branches) and sell them by mail or online to gardeners and curiosity seekers.** A divining rod would also make an interesting and unusual gift. Divining rods help the user to find water.

**761. Be a family relations consultant.** Give advice about how to improve relationships with family members. If you can provide a satisfactory standard of advice your local area should provide you with enough business. There may be licensing requirements for you depending on the advice and scope of your practice.

**762. Start an enterprise which takes local air travelers to the nearest airport with your van,** so that travelers don't have to worry about their cars and long term parking expenses. Plus no one likes to drive to the airport on Get out of town days. Arranging for several travelers in one trip makes this especially more profitable.

**763. Produce a selection of small posters of dogs and cats.** Have these stocked at pet shops and gifts shops. For example, at pet shops have a sample of each poster covered by a transparent plastic? Hang these from a rack and have the saleable posters in rolls in a basket underneath.

**764. Make candid videos of weddings**. Candid videos provide a fascinating, more accurate record of a wedding. Copies can be duplicated and sold to family members. Also do candid videos of parties, promotions, day trips and other special occasions.

**765. Produce a selection of key-rings which have unusual fobs.** For example the fobs might be made from: large flat sea-shells, large foreign coins, circles cut from old LPs, fossils, slate, etc. Sell from a stall at crafts fairs and flea markets.

**766. Organize theme parties for children and teenagers.** You supply the party-goers with simple costumes, food and entertainment. Each party might be related to a popular theme such as science fiction, pirates, witches and wizards, Wild West, etc.

767. **Invent ideas for practical jokes**. Sell these by either producing a regular newsletter or a directory of jokes for different occasions. You might also set up a national practical jokes club. A National Practical Joke Day? Oh yeah, April Fools day.

768. **Create a butterfly online catalog and sell to collectors**. Obtain stock by advertising your interest in buying butterfly collections in collector's magazines. Find wholesale butterfly suppliers from all over the world. Get best pricing on stock and in Plexiglas displays and markup accordingly.

769. **Begin a business which produces horror novelty wall-hangings**. For example, a framed picture which has the picture itself covered by a sliding or hinged door. The door can be opened to reveal a scary scene. Another example would be a wall mirror with the faint face of a ghost peering out. This could be a great Halloween seasonal business.

770. **Compile a guide to educational and leisure holiday courses**. Have this published in book form and sell by mail or online and through bookshops. This has the potential for a successful annual publication.

771. **Start a mail or online firm which sells live insects and bugs and other products related to keeping and breeding insects.** Advice might also be given on what insects to keep. Your service might be called 'Bug Me Please'. Also publish a newsletter with a title like 'Insect Keeper'.

772. **Design and produce a stock market investor's log book.** The purpose of this log book is to record and chart: the prices of individual shares, purchases, sells, expenses, profits and losses. Sell by direct mail to investors and if published in book form, on Amazon and Barnes and Noble.

773. **Produce a series of audio CD's or MP3's which contain quotes from the bible.** The quotes on each CD/MP3 might be selected according to a theme. For example: How to meet bereavement and sorrow, how to meet the challenges of everyday life, and how to live in harmony with others.

774. **Design and produce animation kits for amateur film makers.** Each kit consists of numerous paper characters with moveable joints and a selection of background scenery. An amateur film maker can use a kit to make hobby and animation films. A kit might have, for example, a Wild West or a war theme.

**775. Pay a taxidermist to prepare, stuff and mount fish or other animals**. Produce a mail or online catalog about your mounted animals. Advertise in sports and hunting and fishing publications. Also sell through gift shops and fishing and hunting shops and from you own online website. Take the spread of what you're being paid by your customers and what the taxidermists charges you. Provide extra services like picking up and delivering the finished products.

**776. Start a mail or online business which sells a wide range of dog products** for example, tools and supplies for hunting and fishing,  travel kennels, muzzles, shampoos and conditioners, collars, ornaments, etc., all with a canine theme.

**777. Develop your dog grooming skills** to a professional standard and open your own dog grooming Parlor business.

**778. Use leather to make your own brand of top quality dog collars and leashes**. Personalize it with dog's name on it for that personal feel. Leather is still valued among per owners.

**779. Become a pet portrait photographer.** You have to prove to potential customers that your portraits are far superior to any amateur photographs by simply showing them your photographic catalog. This can be done by displaying your work to the public at craft fairs and through your online store. Approach every school in your area and show them your quality and affordability. Sell your service to people who take a real interest in their animals and who love your work. Developing this niche will create lifelong friends too. Those who love their animals are family members.

780. **Commission artists to do original paintings of horses and horse racing.** Set up a business which distributes and sells these paintings. For example, you might display the paintings in a mobile showroom which visits horse racing and horse show events.

781. **Start a service which makes audio recordings of wedding ceremonies.** Video cameras, often times are not allowed in church or produce poor images. However, discreet microphones can record the ceremony. Copies on CD/MP3 can be sent to friends and relatives at home and overseas.

782. **Set up a business which makes wooden dog kennels in kit form**. Sell by mail or online from ads in dog lovers publications or get them stocked at local pet shops.

783. With the permission of the appropriate authorities, **sell nuts or popcorn in an open space of a city park to passers-by and tourists** who want to feed the pigeons. Or, if at a suitable seaside resort, sell bits of fish to visitors who want to feed the seagulls.

784. Set up an enterprise which **manufactures hutches and coops for chickens, small animals, and birds.** Sell in kit or finished form. Advertise on Craigslist or EBay. Sell also to local feed stores.

785. **Bike Repair Business**. In many parts of the country, this business tends to be seasonal, but you can find ways around that. Rent a storage unit and offer to store people's bicycles over the winter after you do a tune-up and any needed repairs on them. If you want to cater to the ""professional bikers" you can have business all year. These road race riders are training through snow, sleet and dark of night. Some of them work on their own bicycles, but many of them don't, so you can get their business all year. And if you keep Saturday shop hours, you can be sure you will have a group of enthusiasts coming by to talk all things cycling. Work in a bike shop to get training and learn the nuances of bicycle repair.

786. **Create your own Business Plan Service**. Offer a soup-to-nuts business plan, including marketing research, the business plan narrative, the executive summary and the financial statements. Plan your fees around the main point that the client will want and offer the others as add-on services. You can give clients an electronic file and allow them to take it from there, or you can keep the business plan on file and offer the service of tweaking it whenever necessary.

Have business plan samples to show your clients--and make sure to include your own.

**787. Start a business which delivers bulk pet food directly to the public.** Build up a round of regular customers. Call on houses throughout your area to sell your service. Get wholesale from a local supplier. This saves people a lot of time and money.

**788. Begin a business which organizes wildlife observation holidays.** These might be based in a forest, for example, unspoiled coastal area or mountainous region. Produce a brochure and advertise in wildlife magazines. There are many people who would love to go bird watching, for example with others, or what watching on the coast. Advertise in libraries, schools and Craigslist.

**789. Start a second-hand art and book display** and take it to antique markets or fairs. Obtain your stock by placing ads in art or book collector's magazines or Craigslist or other free classified sites. State that you wish to buy collections of second-hand art books and art pieces too.

**790. Open up a Restaurant.** Every town, big or small, needs (and deserves) a few good, quality restaurants. Your local pizza joint won't suffice for all occasions and events. But much like owning a bakery, opening a restaurant is not something to go into half-heartedly. You need to have the passion, the drive, and the obsession of both a great entrepreneur and a chef (or at least a hard-core foodie all willing to work long hours to get your restaurant started and to keep it going. If you have that drive and experience, however, being a restaurateur can be a successful endeavor and a great business for a small town. Just be aware that as glamorous as it might seem from the outside, one-quarter of all restaurants will fail within the first year. We don't say this to discourage you; it's just good to know what you're up against. Doing your market research prior to opening, and investing in technology such as a restaurant POS system, can help you ensure your business stays open and on top.

791. **How about becoming a Chimney Sweep?** Learning to be a chimney sweep may mean nothing more than apprenticing with someone already in the business. By becoming a chimney expert, you can combine a chimney sweep business with a chimney inspection service--covering more than just whether or not the chimney needs cleaning but whether the chimney is in good working order or in need of repair. Work with other technicians that can rebuild and repair them and you've got a complete business. Develop your route of clients.

792. **Sell information and advice about antiques**. Provide clients with a confidential service which identifies and values antiques from descriptions and photographs. Also give

advice about care, cleaning and storage of individual items. Produce flyers about your service. Bring these to antique stores and dealers in your area along with business cards. These owners will be a primary source for leads.

793. **Take a course in basketry**. As you develop your skill slowly begin to sell what you make. When your work reaches a high enough standard, go into business full-time.

794. **Start a paper collecting, shredding and disposal service**. Have impressive flyers and business cards printed to promote your service and send them to businesses.

795. **Create a home-based debt collections service**. Get a job with a debt collection agency and learn all you can before you strike out on your own. At first specialize in one type of trade and, if successful, expand into collecting debts for other trades. Your voice and ability to converse naturally on the phone really helps, along with your organizational skills.

796. **Produce a series of audio CD's or MP3's about Confucianism, Buddhism or Islamism**. Have them stocked at health food shops and bookstores. Or sell online at Amazon or from ads in free online publications.

797. **Design and manufacture business maternity clothes for businesswomen**. Have them stocked in maternity and other women's clothes shops and sell by mail order. Open your own website too to promote your very hot

New clothing segment. Hire others on a piece by piece basis so you can fill larger orders quicker.

798. **Make videos for people who want to sell their small business**. Each video is designed to show a business in its best light. In the video, interview customers, look at its standing in the community, review sales and its numbers etc. Your video should help achieve the highest possible sales price for the businesses whose sale you promote. Maybe call it Business 360.

799. **Write jokes and comedy for profit.** Put together a correspondence course about how to make people laugh. Base this on a method which is your own invention. For example, jokes are like the keys on a piano: there's a limited number but they can be played in an infinity of combinations. Study comedians from your day or from the past and find your niche. Write your jokes to that audience. As you get good at this, either take your act to the stage, or write for sitcoms. Where this goes is entirely up to you and your ability to write.

800. **Publish a blog about successful management**. Aim the editorial at managers in large corporations. Each post should discuss the issues relevant to the manager of today who wants to succeed.

801. **Professional Researcher correspondence course** which gives instruction about becoming anything research.

With search engines today providing billions of pieces of information accessed immediately, researcher have a new found power in the world of information management. This course would appeal to those who would like a career in this field and to authors and new reporters who want to do their own research. Sell from ads in literary publications, bookstores and on Craigslist.

802. **Produce uplifting bookmarkers** which have attractive embroidered designs. Package them in cellophane and have them stocked at bookshops.

803. **Publish a weekly "Thrifty Nickel-type" publication** for your local community which specializes in real estate, car sales, garage sales etc. Have business listings and advertising pay for the publication. Distribute to every retailer in the community. Make it easy and affordable to buy an ad. Know your cost per page to produce it and support it with advertising.

804. **Write and publish a book about how to cut the cost of a wedding.** Alternatively write and produce a manual about how to have a beautiful, big wedding on a shoestring. Have it stocked in bookshops and boutiques or sell from ads in wedding magazines and on Amazon for larger distribution.

**805. Design and manufacture wooden kits for constructing motorized model boats.** Run sailing derbies at local ponds and pools. Sell from ads in hobby magazines or have them stocked in modelling and crafts shops.

**806. Use direct mail to sell model steam engines** to engineers, doctors, scientists, company directors and other professional people.

**807. Set up a mail or online business which specializes in selling videos, films, photographs, posters and slides about the pop music culture.** Use your ingenuity to find products, for example canvass picture libraries and record and film companies.

**808. Write and publish a newsletter, online blog or YouTube channel which is devoted to profitable hobbies.** The newsletter will be aimed at those who are looking for both an interesting new hobby and a way of making extra money. Asses the profit potential of a wide range of hobbies.

**809. Become an advertising consultant.** There has never been a time in history where maximizing your advertising dollars has been more needed than now.

Assessing the business owner's needs, budget and what kind of results they desire, and then allocating the ad dollars in that area to maximize the ROI (return on investment), is the primary concern of the ad consultant.

810. **Start a service which organizes the painting of murals** in bedrooms, dining rooms, residential games rooms, etc. Advertise in up-market publications.

811. **Call door-to-door and offer to take top quality passport photographs**. Take the photographs in the customer's house. Someone returns at a later date to deliver the photographs and collect payment. All family members might have their photos taken for passports, ID cards, bus and train passes, etc.

812. **Create Life-Sized Train.** Make a train from a riding lawnmower (make it look like a train) and make 3 or 4 passenger cars that you can give rides at fairs, church Halloween parties, and summer events. Great for photos of children also. Rent it for $100+ an hour.

813. **Dental, Bank and Office Cleaning Service**. There are many directions you can take this business. If you want to work during hours when no one else does, you can focus on dental offices, legal firms, business offices and bank clients. You can focus on retail businesses and keep your customers clumped into one or two blocks. Restaurants are in great need

of daily thorough cleaning and can be a great source of steady clients. Perhaps you would be more interested in house cleaning. Many times with cleaning services you don't have to spend lots of money on advertising or marketing because your customers will come by word of mouth. Flyers, letters and Craigslist initially targeting dental and legal offices can get you started.

814. **Produce colored acetate paper printed with painting by number designs for shops.** The designs could include elaborate 'sale' signs and pictures with a Christmas theme. A shopkeeper sticks the acetate sheets to one side of a window and paints the design or picture on the other.

815. **Begin a firm which produces and distributes a range of I'm in love' products.** These will include T-shirts, car stickers, signs and badges.

816. **Bring out a board game about buying and running a retail business, a rock band, a pet store, a fast food restaurant.** The game might be a game store special or it might involve several types of businesses. Sell from ads in publications which list businesses for sale. Also from your own website and Craigslist.

817. **Rent out model trains or slot cars to enthusiasts**. This service would allow enthusiasts to examine and use a wide range of trains and slot cars. You could include an option for the customer to buy if they are particularly fond of any model.

818. **Make simple wooden footstools** - up to twelve inches in height, for standing on to reach things from shelves. Sell through local shops.

819. **Make Large Mailboxes.** Contact the owners of houses with small mail boxes and offer to supply and install a large mail box. Have some handmade designs that rock.

820. **Fireplace Fire DVD with Christmas Music.** Bring out a DVD or MP4 which consists of a long recording (2 hours) of an open fire with Christmas music in the background. Expand the selection by having a 432 Hz (God Frequency) music in the back ground too for healing and health. By playing the DVD or MP4 anyone can have the charm of an open fire in their home without the mess, hassle and cleanup and receive a relaxing musical background to boot.

821. **Make peg abacuses**. Each abacus is a wooden block which has rows of dots instead of beads. A row has one peg to indicate the value of that row. Package these and sell as either a children's educational aid or a novelty gift for adults.

Make wooden clocks also to teach kids how to tell time. Make them beautiful, functional and collectible so that families will want to keep them and pass them down to their family members.

822. **Craft Business Development.** Write and produce a course about how to start and build a successful craft business. Subjects covered by the course might include: How to choose and design a winning product, how to sell Craft work, how to use other craft workers in your business, etc. Have you been to **www.etsy.com** lately? It's grown up now. Many amazing ideas.

823. **Have a yard, garage or a porch? Hold a special sale.** Raise extra cash by displaying your unwanted items at your sale. Invite others in the neighborhood also to sell their merchandise to bring additional customers to the area. Place homemade directional signs around the area and advertise in Craigslist and other free classified sites.

824. **Set up a business where you sell non-fiction business books.** This type of business offers a great potential for profit if you publish the books you write and sell. Start with EBooks and graduate to paperbacks. Amazon has a great program for new writers. Learn their system and thrive.

**825. Business Consultants do very well**. To be a consultant, you need to have an expertise in something so you can market yourself as an advisor to others, looking to work in that arena. Perhaps you managed several large warehouses in your career with a drugstore company, you did all the marketing for many years for a large shoe manufacturer or you set up a chain of beauty supply stores or fast food restaurants. You can use this experience to help others do similar things without making the same mistakes that you made along the way.

**826. Be an EBay Sales Pro**. Do you have items lurking around your household that you could sell on eBay? Figure out your asking price and decide whether to auction it or put it in your eBay store. Then decide if you want a minimum bid and how long you want the auction to last. You will want to establish a PayPal account to use for transactions. The eBay website provides all the information you need to know to get up and running with an eBay business. Create a business by selling "in-demand" products yourself and turn them quickly or sell for others and take 25-30% of the sale as a commission to sell their items for them.

**827. Put together a course about how to become a professional investment adviser**. Get appropriate licensing in your area. Sell through ads in the financial press.

828. **Learn the craft of woodcarving**. When you become skilled earn money from carving popular first names in relief and turn these into brooches. Also turn out other carved Jewelry such as pendants, bracelets and earrings.

829. **Produce Christmas cards** which are printed on the front with, for example, "Happy Christmas from the Smith Family". Or, instead of the name 'Smith', pick one of the dozens of other popular surnames. Sell packs of these cards by direct mail to people listed in telephone directories.

830. **Use sea-shells to make a range of Jewelry, including sea-shell brooches, bracelets, earrings and necklaces.** Place these on racks and have them stocked at suitable shops.

831. **Make money from renting out expensive children's toys**. The toys you rent out will include remote controlled models and computerized games. Use a little van to deliver the toys to customers. Paint in toy town color scheme. Call the van a toy mobile or similar suitable name.

832. **Begin a direct mail or mail or online business which sells crafts books to craft workers**. Buy books from publishers, buy manuscripts from authors and publish these yourself, or write a craft book which has universal appeal and sell this.

833. **There seems to be an insatiable demand for quality, novel or inexpensive clocks.** If you want to start an import business, this may be a suitable area to try. Check out Alibaba.com for ideas.

834. **Begin a business which produces a syndicated online catalog**. Most catalogs consist of the goods of one firm. A syndicated catalog could have details of products from hundreds of suppliers. Try to keep the suppliers exclusive and charge for these companies to be in your publication.

835. **Flea Market Sales**. People love to spend weekends rummaging through tables full of other people's unwanted items, looking for treasures. Make sure to change your layout and put new stuff out for sale often. You want people to come back time and again to see what's new. You don't even have to have that much new stuff to make things look new. Just moving an item from a table to the top of a bookshelf might get it noticed, even though the item has been in your inventory since you first started having sales. Ask family members for their "treasures" too. If you have some wholesale connections you can market new things every week too. Items like sunglasses, t-shirts, ball caps, knives, art items and crafts always seem to sell well.

836. **Become a Golf Coach**. If you love golf, why not combine your golf skills with your business. Let the local public courses know about your coaching business. Cultivate

relationships with the staff and encourage them to recommend you as a coach. Every club these days has a professional golf pro. Golfing is a game that business people use to develop relationships outside the office. You do need to be a better than average golfer to develop a reputation as a golf coach. You also need to be a good teacher, know how to be motivational and be willing to work with many different types of players. Coaching can be really fun and very rewarding.

837. **In a large city operate a telephone information service for amateur photographers.** Photographers who subscribe to your service can telephone you to get a list of today's photo opportunities. For example: a film star arriving at an airport and a record breaking attempt.

838. **Set up a mail or online business which sells kits for making leather products.** For example, kits for wallets, check book covers and book covers. Design and manufacture the kits yourself and produce an online catalog.

839. **Create a course about palmistry and tarot.** Sell from ads in astrology magazines. One attraction of the course is that the palmist and tarot skills learned could be used to make money.

840. **Compile and publish a book of sales messages, phrases, selling points and closes**. The format of this book might be tips and hacks on how to close sales in any industry. Businesses are potential buyers are everywhere. Sell through your own website or publish your book and sell on Amazon or Barnes and Noble.

841. **Energy Auditor.** Homeowners are always on the lookout for ways to save on their utility bills. You can come to their aid by providing them with an audit of their house and giving them a breakdown of how they could accomplish real savings in heating, cooling and electrical use. You can go one step further and do the implementation and installation of some of your suggestions in their home yourself. Do a complete appliance audit, with efficiency ratings and calculations based on the age of the appliance. And don't forget the water heater!

842. **Devise a program which is designed to make a person more dynamic**. A more dynamic, confident person has a greater chance of achieving success in life, the career they desire etc. Publish your program and sell it by direct mail, business opportunity seekers and those searching for that special job.

843. **Buy a portable children's mini-railway**. Children can sit on the carriages and are taken up and down a short track. Hire out your railway for fund raising at fairs and money-making tourist sites.

844. **Become a Home Inspector.** In order to be successful as a home inspector, you will want to establish contacts with real estate agents, investors and bankers who can recommend your services to customers. The home inspection field is one where you will need to do constant updating of your education and knowledge. New products are constantly coming out on the market--if you only know about decks made of wood, you will not know how to inspect and assess the new materials on the market, such as composites that are made to look like real wood. Also keep apprised of all safety updates of materials and issues with things like off-gassing, carbon monoxide production, and other chemical precautions. In most cities Home Inspectors get $300-$450 per inspection complete with photos of the home and areas of concern. Most states now have a minimum requirement for hours (2000 in some states) on the job doing inspections with a journeyman. Check your state for requirement.

845. **Start a publishing enterprise which specializes in producing quality hand printed poetry books**. Get these stocked at bookshops, card shops and sell by mail to poetry lovers.

846. **Devise and produce an easy-to-use system for cataloging coin collections.** Sell this through stamp and coin shops, or from ads in collector's magazines.

847. **International Marketing and Law.** As the emphasis on global business and trade grows, organizations will be looking for individuals who will have the education, experience, and skill set to navigate areas like international marketing, law, tax codes, work and environmental regulations, and even morals and ethics. Individuals who want to take advantage of this trend will likely need a law degree with an emphasis on international law or an international MBA. Excellent communication skills, as well as knowledge and/or fluency in one or more languages will also help. Individuals who follow this path should also be willing to live in several different countries over the course of their careers, as this will be a future trend.

848. **Publish a book or blog for people who want to become children's authors.** In each issue include advice and information which will help children's authors to get work accepted for publication.

849. **Produce and launch a course which teaches people how to write fiction for adolescents for profit.** Fiction writing is still the number one genre of books sold every day at Amazon.

**850. Create a website of old TV and movie scripts.** There is obviously a lot of skill involved in writing a TV or movie script and there are numerous people who would be willing to pay to learn and have the copies of those scripts to show off to their friends.

**851. Publish poetry in a way similar to music sheets.** On a printed folded sheet feature a main poem and maybe 3 or 4 support poems. Get these 'poem sheets' stocked at bookshops and newsagents. The price might be the same as a daily newspaper. Also organize a chart of top selling poem sheets.

**852. Use classified ads to sell a selection of English language newspapers and magazines to the world.** Buyers will include those who are curious about what English language newspapers and magazines are like.

**853. Information Technology.** Think of all the technology we didn't have just a few decades ago, a decade ago, a few years ago, last year! Computers, the Internet, and Smartphones have changed the way we do business and communicate with the world and our customers. And it will continue to do so for the foreseeable future. As more technology is developed, IT professionals such as programmers, security specialists, and administrators will continue to be in high demand.

If college is in your future, you've got to at least consider this career path. With technology advances and it changing all the time, who knows where this will take you?

854. **Begin a gift service which provides a nostalgic selection of magazines from the month of a person's birth.** Advertise your service in the columns or classified ads which feature other gift ideas.

855. **Set up a mail or online business which sells casting equipment, supplies and books.** Potential customers include a wide range of craft workers and hobbyists. Begin by learning everything you can about small scale casting then track down trade suppliers of products related to casting.

856. **Devise and invent puzzles and word games**. Sell these through specialist magazines and newspapers and to book publishers.

857. **Teach Skiing and Snowboarding**. Teach two of the most popular winter sports at ski resorts, either as a ski instructor hired by the resort, or as an independent ski or snowboard instructor.

858. **Compile and publish a bulletin that informs subscribers of photography** competitions they are eligible to enter in this country and around the world. Advertise in photograph magazines.

**859. Set up a mail or online business which is devoted to selling products designed to increase a person's attractiveness to the opposite sex.** Products might include books, CD's or MP3's, courses, systems and aids.

**860. At a tourist site earn money from painting a person's name on a print.** The name thus becomes part of the picture. For example, there might be a hoarding of posters in your picture and a person's name becomes one of the posters. Design and produce the prints yourself.

**861. Produce an aerial video of your area.** Duplicate this and have it stocked at video hire shops and other local shops.

**862. Publish a newsletter about human interest stories, unusual facts, interesting paragraphs, etc.** Subscribers would include people who produce their own, regular, amateur publication. They would use your newsletter as a source to provide fillers for their own publication.

**863. English Improvement.** Start a school of English and give lessons to a group or individual who wants to improve their written and spoken English. You might give lessons either in your own home or online via Skype or FaceTime. English as a second language in the US is a growing need, especially in Border States and high population cities.

864. **Start a dating agency or marriage bureau especially for the divorced or never been married over 40 group.** Use local advertising to attract clients. Promote your online website. It's the easiest, safest and fastest way to date today.

865. **Begin a business which specializes in organizing romantic getaways and holidays.** Arrange for courting couples, newly-weds and mature couples to have getaways at hunting lodges, cottages and bed and breakfast locations and castles.

866. **Earn a living from teaching people how to find a lover or life partner.** You could hold classes in a conference room or a restaurant. Produce an audio CD/MP3 course, and give lessons.

867. **Produce painting by numbers outlines specially designed for hobbyists.** For example, do outlines of locomotives, or background scenery for railway modelers. Sell these from ads in hobby magazines or get them stocked at modelling shops.

868. **Household or Office Organizer.** You can choose either to do the organizing work or to come in to a home or business and consult on the things that the owner could do to better organize. Have a portfolio of different organizational ideas and scenarios in different rooms in the home or business

and talk with the home or business owner about the style he or she likes. Create checklists and questionnaires to understand how the family and associates uses the space. This would likely be a contractual one-off project, but can be very lucrative as well.

869. **Uplifting Business Posters.** Organize an online catalog which has a wide range of uplifting business posters and frame them. The posters might be about: inspiring, sales efficiency, hard work and saving energy. Send the catalog to businesses and offices in your community. Branch out from there.

870. **Become a part of the world's largest travel club,** WorldVentures. I'm involved with this and love it. Huge savings on travel, hotels, airfare, car rentals and even earn travel dollars (bonus bucks) by eating out at restaurants and attending sporting events. Best part? Your savings at hotels, airfare, etc. is guaranteed to save you money. And every dollar you spend on your membership is used for your travel! Unreal. WV is now in over 30+ countries worldwide. Do you want to build an amazing income too? Just tap in and build a huge network of business partners and earn a solid 5, 6 or 7-figure income. Many are doing that right now, and so can you. Start slow and build it part-time. Travel the world while building your business. We'll even help you build it! Check out this link for more information. **https://bit.ly/2HTsg2W.**

871. **Begin a venture which arranges for business and sales meetings to take place at exotic and unusual venues**. For example, a businessman can negotiate a contract with a client at a castle, or on a yacht or in a sightseeing plane. Maybe combine this with your WorldVentures membership, and double-dip?

872. **Put together a range of uplifting, Bible and spoken word audio CD's or MP3's.** Have them stocked in video rental shops and rented out or sell online at your store.

873. **Make badges with a badge-a-minute press** and sell badges to local businesses, political candidates and their followers, sports teams and schools.

874. **Set up a business which organizes the occult, massage, rocks and crystals, palm readers and mediums.** Find a venue, sell 10'x10' spaces to host it. County Fair locations are always great and central to a county and parking is never a problem. Advertise it a lot by placing ads everywhere. Publicize and sell tickets online through PayPal. Also promote through Social media like FaceBook and Instagram and Craigslist to attract potential attendees and vendors. Always fun in early October to catch the Halloween and Christmas shoppers.

875. **Sell Funny Hats.** Attend pop concerts, festivals, fairs and other large public events and sell funny hats, baseball caps and t-shirts. There's a great mark-up and can keep allow you learning what sells best to open up your own Etsy or Shopify account.

876. **Start a theatrical play of the month club.** Operate this like a book club but sell only theatrical plays. The club will not offer discounts on publications, but you can send copies of the latest plays opening at theatres.

877. **Sell Jazz memorabilia by mail or online.** Start a world-wide search for products to put in your catalog. The products might include: photographs, slides, posters, old magazines, duplicate press cuttings, books, video and audio CD's or MP3's.

878. **Interior Decorator.** Market your decorating skills and talents to building contractors. People purchasing new homes can often be overwhelmed with the choices and possibilities in home decorating. Design a questionnaire for each major element and each major room in the house. Find out how the homeowner will use the home--are there children? Pets? Does the woman of the house wear high heels? Do the home's residents neglect to remove shoes? How will each room be used? Where might task lighting and ambient lighting be most appropriate?

What kinds of furniture and decorating styles match the homeowners? Depending on the scope of the decorating, many interior decorators make six-figure incomes. It's largely a referral based business.

**879. Sell unusual musical instruments from your own online catalog.** For example: folk music instruments from Third World countries, and early musical instruments.

**880. During the Christmas season, form a group of carol singers.** Hire this group out to parties, restaurants, night clubs and cruise lines.

**881. Bring out folders specially designed to hold sheet music or knitting patterns**. Sell these from either, suitable shops or ads in publications read by people who collect sheet music or knitting patterns.

**882. Make fashionable patchwork sweaters** and have them stocked at shops. Alternatively, sell the sweaters or funky patch jeans from a booth at a market fair.

**883. Start a school for pop or rock group management**. Your students will include those who aspire to become a manager or need an agent or group manager. The market are leaders of a pop or rock group and those desiring to be group managers/agents. The course might be taught holding classes.

884. **Put together a service which sells personalized: golf balls, tennis balls, etc.** The exact method of placing names or initials on the balls can be worked out. As you provide this service, you could create a lucrative market waiting to be exploited. Personalization is still a great business.

885. **Design and manufacture kits for making models with sticks**, for example: model churches, castles, windmills, houses, etc. Buy the cocktail or Popsicle sticks in their unpacked state from the manufacturer. Sell your kits by mail or online from ads in craft magazines or distribute to model shops.

886. **Write and publish a website which is about how to sell simple information**. In each blog/vlog suggest new ideas for the kind of information which can be sold. Also review the latest offerings by other information sellers. Put it all together in a course and sell it to a world market.

887. Write a book or create an audio CD/MP3 which has a title like: **'How to Set a World Record'**. Include information about how to get a record accepted and give ideas about feats which might be attempted. Sell through bookshops or Amazon.

888. **Design and make collector's doll's clothes** for collectors or manufacturers of dolls. Either make the clothes to order or produce an online catalog which gives full detail of your range and what you do.

889. **Notary Public**. In most states in the U.S., a notary public is a state officer who is authorized to witness and attest to the legalities of certain documents by signature and stamping a seal. Most states require that you pass an exam and a background check. It costs very little to become a notary and your income from notary work is negligible. And it is not a big moneymaking venture! Many states set the fees you can charge for Notary services. Notaries can add additional fees, and often do, including travel and hourly rates for additional meetings such as rehearsals, other prep time and any special requests.

890. **Design and make, or import, kimonos**. Sell by your online website or get them stocked at suitable retailers. Importing them from Indonesia and China are very cost effective with a 10x markup potential. Lots of room for retailer profits and yours. If you create an online store, you'll keep more of the profits too by cutting out the retailer. Import them from Indonesia or Southeast Asia for $2.00 and sell in the US for $20.00.

891. **Start a mail or online business which sells startup kits for being an amateur musician** including instructions on how to play a particular instrument. Include also shortcuts and hacks on learning that instrument. Include starting music that can be practiced by the buyer. Put the kits together from products which are already on the market.

892. **Begin a business which makes cushions of unusual shapes**. For example: star shaped, heart shaped, horseshoe shaped, or round with a hole in the middle. Market online. These are great accent pieces for sofas too.

893. **Personal Concierge**. This business is for someone who is supremely efficient and has the ability to make things happen. People who hire you will expect things when they want them and you need to be able to come through with not only what they want, but with a personal touch and a smile on your face. The most likely clients for a personal concierge service are top executives who find themselves at the office by 7 a.m. and are there most nights until 9 p.m., leaving them very little time to do all those things that often need to be done during those very hours.

894. **Personal Trainer**. Advertise your services in places where everyone goes, like gyms, restaurants and grocery stores. Having a website is a good idea--people want some privacy in their decision-making when it comes to getting fit.

They can go to your website and determine if your approach to personal training is an approach that would work for them. It is important to emphasize the safety aspect of using a personal trainer. You can help clients get fit and avoid injury too. Personal trainers often make $20-$50 an hour for their services.

**895. Property Manager.** Your job, in the case of rental units, will be to make sure the property is running smoothly and that rents are collected. For seasonal properties, you will most likely spend your management time making sure the property is ready for seasonal visits and well-maintained when no one is around. If the owners go away for six weeks in the winter, the property manager makes regular checks on the property. You will be the contact number if the security system operator needs to contact someone about a breach in security. Managers are often couples too, and a real estate license is required in most states.

**896. Small Engine Repair & Lawnmower Blade Sharpening.** If you are handy and love mechanics and sharp lawnmower blades, this job's for you. Most community colleges offer some level of engine-repair courses. Another way to learn would be to take a part-time position at a repair shop or a rental facility where you could learn on the job and receive the training. You should be prepared to work on push lawn mowers, riding lawn mowers, generators, garden tools such as rototillers and edger equipment, chainsaws, wood chippers and snow blowers. You need to decide whether you'll want to take on bigger jobs, such as tractors, snowmobiles and ATVs; space may be your decision-maker.

**897. Start a children's educational video sale website.** A selection of DVD's should be offered for each age group. Produce a catalog about your videos and advertise your rental service in a wide range of publications.

**898. Solar Energy Consultant.** You meet with homeowners and conduct a home inspection and give clients a report on their solar options for their particular home and site. This can range from full-fledged general solar installations that generate electricity to simple solar walkway lighting. You might want to start by working in a solar products company to become knowledgeable in the solar energy field. However, to be a consultant, it is often best not to be affiliated with any one company or product and be able to recommend products and options across the field of solar energy. On the other hand, working for a local solar company can give you motivation, training and a regular paycheck. Still an industry looking to grow.

**899. Design and make kits for making soft toy dolls.** Teach others how to design, make, sell and market their toys. Place ads in craft magazines and sell from your online store.

900. **Temp Jobs.** When you are new to the marketplace, or reentering the workforce or you're seeking a temporary position that can fit around your school and family schedule, perhaps you could seek out a "temp agency" that can help you find a part-time or full-time position. Many times, a temp job at a local business, turns into a fulltime job with benefits and an opportunity to work more hours and grow with that company. There are dozens of temp agencies in large cities and generally several in small towns. Good labor is always hard to find. Be found and apply today with your local temp agency and let them help you find the perfect position.

901. **Add a stand to fragments of original rock from Mount Everest** and sell through gift shops or ads in mountaineering publications. You might also do the same for other major mountains like Half Dome in Yosemite, for example or Mt. McKinley. Buy the glass displays wholesale and sell the displays at craft stores, flea markets and craft fairs.

902. **Entrepreneur Training.** Produce an audio CD/MP3 course or education course about becoming an entrepreneur. The potential market includes the hundreds of thousands of people who start their own business each year and who would like to get your take on how to do it right. Teach students also, how to organize an IPO (Initial Public Offering) and where to get capital and sales to start and grow their business.

903. **Used Book Sales**. Do you have a few dozen boxes of books stashed away in the house somewhere? Why not make a business out of them? In order to gain customers--especially repeat customers--you will need to have some regular shop hours. Make your shop known for something-a specific category or two of books, having some first editions for sale, all paperbacks a dollar and all hardcovers two bucks, and/or a swap program. Maps, illustrations, postcards, greeting cards, t-shirts and magazines are good sidelines to include in your shop. Another profitable way to sell books is on EBay and Amazon. Charge the required $3.99 for shipping and handling on what the sales price is and you should do ok.

904. **Become a Wedding Planner.** You will need to be up-to-date on wedding trends and fads, dress styles, color trends--almost everything under the sun! Subscribe to Bridal magazines. Ask questions. Offer your customers an ala-carte menu of services, from helping pick flowers, the wedding gown and bridesmaid dresses, the wedding cake selection to picking the venue and hiring the caterer. Before you open your business, shop at all the wedding shops, and even pretend you are a bride-to-be to see what kinds of services the wedding gown shop provides and how they treat potential customers. You need to know every detail of the business to give the accurate impression that you are the go-to person for anyone planning a wedding.

**905. Open a school of computing.** Rent an office and teach or employ others to teach courses about computing. The most financially rewarding courses would be those which help students to get jobs in computing.

**906. Bring out an audio CD/MP3 library of limericks.** This might be produced for children or young adults. Have the CD's or MP3's stocked at bookshops, toy stores and your online store.

**907. Appliance Repairman.** Every household has a number of appliances, large and small that breakdown over time. You can work on your own or on contract with appliance stores to cover their warranty service calls--or, best of all, you can do some of each. Plan to start slow and build your customer base on recommendations and referrals based on work well done. Consider developing relationships with building contractors to be the go-to person to install appliances in newly constructed houses.

**908. Math & Computing Made Easy.** If you have advanced knowledge of mathematics or computing, make an income from teaching students directly in classes or one on one. This is one of the biggest needs in America today, to have qualified math and science students prepared to meet the needs of a technology based society and fill jobs that will be associated with it. Advertise locally. Provide financing for parents and their students.

909. **Carpet Cleaning.** There are millions of homeowners and renters that need their carpets cleaned a few times each year. The proper presentation and pricing, combined with a quality job well done can be the key to your success. Direct mail, Craigslist, flyers and word of mouth is a great way to get the word out about your business.

910. **Contest and Sweepstakes.** You don't have to be lucky to win...just persistent. Many sweepers make full time incomes by entering every contest they can (as often as the rules allow them too). Check out a couple of these sites. **Intouchweekly.com,** and even **software that reminds you, www.sweeperschoice.com**, to enter and then automatically fills in your name and send it off for you. This is a business when you get it going. Why not try it?

911. **Design and produce a selection of astrological badges** for each star sign. Place these badges on cards or boards and distribute them to suitable retailers.

912. **Sports Trip Organizer**. Start an enterprise which organizes trips to sporting events, boxing contests, motor race car or NASCAR competitions, baseball or football games, etc. Your service provides the tickets and the transportation and parking. You might, for example, pay a shopkeeper to open a ticket office in his or her shop and give them a percentage of the ticket cost.

**913. Earn an income from doing artistic hedge cutting.** Advertise in the local press and in newsstand windows. Build up a list of regular customers who need their artistic hedges maintained. I can see it now..."The Hedge Fun Guy!" Sorry.

**914. Moving Service.** Lots of people who are moving want to hire someone to do the heavy lifting for them. You can leave the large-scale, long-distance moving to the big moving companies. Your work can be the local, moving-across-town or to the town-next-door jobs. These are the ones that people start off thinking perhaps they could do themselves, and it will be your job to convince them otherwise. Your signs around town will tempt them to let you take care of that part of the move, while they are busy taking care of those other 500 items on their list.

**915. Start an enterprise which organizes arts and crafts fairs.** Find suitable venues, rent spaces to artists and craft workers. Publicize throughout the local area.

**916. Learn about the craft of making ornaments.** Make money from what you learn by bringing together a selection of supplies for selling to craft hobbyists. Add to this, doing sculpting and molding with clay that can be fired and painted. Craft shops like these seem to be a dying breed but can be very profitable if properly promoted. Crafts are still big business and so much fun.

917. **Hemming and Sewing Business.** Whether you're making onesies and quilts for sale online or at local markets or doing repairs and alterations for locals with ill-fitting clothes, your sewing machine could be your ticket to a work-from-home business. Sewing is truly a lost art. Money for hemming and alterations has gone up dramatically in recent years. Cash in now.

918. **Open a school of antique restoration**. Offer potential students a choice of courses covering most aspects of restoration. Potential students will include antique collectors and dealers. Advertise in magazines about antiques and in antique stores in your area.

919. **Build Homemade Furniture.** Everyone loves a well-built and handmade piece of furniture. If you're already spending time in your workshop, why not sell your wares? Etsy is an excellent place to start selling without having to have a physical storefront. Make outdoor furniture or get fancy with indoor "barnwood" creations.

920. **Alternative Energy.** Don't say good-bye to oil and gas quite yet, but alternative energies such as solar power, wind power, hydrogen power, and geothermal power will create dozens of new careers, from mechanics and plant managers to scientists, engineers, and even sales and marketing professionals, as these energies become more mainstream.

921. **Become a Taxidermist.** Today's world of taxidermy isn't exclusive to preserving real animal specimens. Taxidermy also refers to recreating a specimen using completely artificial materials. Taxidermy schools where you can learn the trade are located almost throughout the country, typically as courses over several weeks specializing in certain levels of expertise, from beginner to master's level. Like any enterprise, there are taxidermy conventions that you can attend and learn about the latest techniques and materials.

922. **Cosmetology and Hairstylist.** Hairstyling is a popular business. Generally a home based hairstylist business is likely to be started by someone who has already has a cosmetology license and career and wants a change. If you already have your cosmetology training and license, and loads of experience under your belt working in a hairstyling salon, you probably have a following that will follow you right home without any hesitation. Good business, long hours, decent pay but that's world of glamor.

923. **Start a craft business which makes enameled products** such as key-ring fobs, earrings, brooches, pendants, Jewelry boxes, boxes for knickknacks, etc. Sell your craftwork from a stall at markets or fairs. Or if your work is of a very high standard sell it through gift shops.

**924. Package pressed flowers.** Each packet might contain an individual set, or unsorted selection, of pressed flowers. Attach the packets to display cards, or place in a display box and distribute to arts and crafts shops.

**925. Design, produce and distribute your own brand of anti-smoking ashtray.** For example, produce an ashtray which is either, a model of a cancerous lung or printed with the names of people who died on the same day from lung cancer. These are sold to people who live with smokers and who they wish would quit smoking. Very niche business.

**926. Start a business which designs and manufactures DIY kits for building small garden swimming pools, decks and backyard bird baths.** Offer buyers a selection of sizes and sell through ads in DIY magazines.

**927. Organize weekend courses for DIY enthusiasts.** Provide students with practical tuition about various popular DIY projects from crafts, to work working projects, to home-remodeling. Advertise in DIY magazines, Craigslist and free online classified sites.

**928. Be an E-Book Author.** Book Publishing is dying; long live the e-reader! Now that anyone can have their work e-published, it is possible for anyone to make a fortune off their writing. The biggest recent example is the **50 SHADES OF**

**GREY** trilogy, but there are many authors taking advantage of the ease of e-publishing. If you love to write and are willing to do your own promotion (and having a blog can really help in that case), writing an e-book is an excellent way to make money at home. Start with writing about what really interest you. You stories or non-fiction can easily be promoted with Amazon or Barnes and Noble. Promote to all your friends too on social media. They will love your book.

929. **Bring together a selection of supplies for making string puppets and start a mail or online business.** There is already a thriving market in doll making supplies. Your business will hopefully divert some people from making dolls to making string puppets.

930. **Start a service which commissions artists to do drawings of business premises or private residences.** Also arrange for the drawings to be reproduced on: stationery, postcards, calendars, business cards, etc. Advertise in business publications and also do work for established printers.

931. **Call Center Representative.** Believe it or not, it is possible to actually make really good money from home when you are a call customer service representative. If you've got a phone line and an internet connection, you can work from home as a call center rep. Median salary: $30,460.

**932. Produce a series of booklets or audio CD's or MP3's about ideas for saving a variety of things.** For example: 'Ideas for Saving Money', 'Ideas for Saving Time', 'Ideas for Saving You the Trouble of Dieting', etc. Sell by mail or online as a complete set.

**933. Produce a course on cartooning.** Pay a skilled cartoonist to devise the course.

**934. If you have the artistic ability to become a cartoon caricaturist**, earn money from doing amusing portraits at a thoroughfare of a shopping or tourist area. Or do caricatures outside football grounds on match day, at festivals, concerts, exhibitions, etc.

**935. Compile and publish a year-book or 'Yellow Pages' type directory for those who want to start a business.** Add a "Christian flavor to it to niche your business too. In the directory list, for example: sources of finance, small business advisers, franchise companies, etc. Also sell advertising space to business opportunities promoters.

**936. Learn the art of calligraphy.** When you become a skilled calligrapher earn money from teaching others in your own home or at evening class.

937. **Start a home party hire service.** The hosts of children's and adults' parties hire from you: chairs, tables, cutlery, plates, glasses, barbecues, etc. Advertise your service either in local newspapers or newsstand's windows. Provide a free delivery service.

938. **Provide a sales service for oil and acrylic painters**. Sell the work of artists by finding outlets and take a commission on all sales. Outlets might include: antiques shops, gift shops, private art exhibitions, overseas shops, art galleries, etc.

939. **Bring out a selection of posters which are packed with biblical quotes**. Sell these through religious bookshops and by mail to schools and practicing Christians. Have your own website too.

940. **Set up a promotional sheet music publishing business**. People who write music and lyrics would find it easier to sell their compositions if they were published. Published compositions could then be circulated to people in the music business.

941. **Debt Collection Business.** It takes a very thick skin to go into this business, but debt collectors only need a telephone and a computer to work, making it a great work-at-home business. It's also a recession-proof (or even recession-loving)

business. Licensing requirements vary from state to state, so make sure you do your homework before setting up shop. Median salary: $31,300.

942. **Set up a business which sells gardening equipment and supplies**. You might, for example, hold the parties in gardens during the afternoons. Once you have developed a successful presentation and range of products, increase the size of your business by recruiting agents.

943. **Start a personalized spring-water bottling and distribution business.** Advertise for someone who owns a property which has a natural spring water supply. Negotiate a contract with the owner which allows you to bottle and sell the spring water. Personalize the labels for businesses, weddings, sports teams etc.

944. **Green Consulting.** Many smaller companies would like to find ways to make their business processes greener without spending more green. You can help them to figure out ways to improve their carbon footprint without sacrificing the bottom line.

945. **Write and publish a manual which has a title like 'How to Start Your Own Mail or online business'.** Use classified ads and direct mail to sell this to business opportunity seekers.

946. **Be a Ventriloquist**. Set up a mail or online business which sells books and products related to ventriloquism. Produce booklets and CD's or MP3's which give instructions about ventriloquism and ideas for stage acts. Also sell props and dummies. Do your own routine too for side money on stage.

947. **Bring out an 'ideas, characters and plots' newsletter for writers**. In each issue suggest ideas for: locations, characters, events, phrases, use of words, etc. One of the main selling points of your newsletter is that it will help a writer to become a published author.

948. **Help people to get jobs by starting Resume & Cover Letter design service**. Conduct your own research into what information a resume and cover letter should have that impresses employers. Basically, it is professionally printed and presents the most important facts about a person's career history in a simple, clear way that gets the job!

949. **Create a website that provides "well written toast" for the Groom's Best Man and Bride' Maid** as they toast the newlyweds at the reception dinner. Charge for individual toasts or create one individually prepared one for more.

**950. Begin a mail or online business which promotes the hobby of collecting currency notes.** Put together a catalog which lists a wide selection of currency notes and collecting accessories. Advertise in coin collecting magazines.

**951. Start a business which sells novel birth and death certificates** to those who like to claim that they had previous lives. Design the certificates yourself and pay for them to be printed. Also offer a service which uses occult methods to identify previous lives. Selling through a website is easiest too.

**952. Publish an 'ideas' photo newsletter for photographers.** Focus the attention of the newsletter on ideas for saleable photographs. Use ads in photography magazines to sell subscriptions and emphasize that the newsletter aims to help people to earn money from photography.

**953. Make home-made chocolates.** Rent a corner of an established shop on a Saturday to sell them. Sell at fairs and flea markets too. Make them irresistible. Packaging them in small boxes does just the. Brand them and seek out gift basket manufacturers to sell to, the rest of the week.

**954. Website Beta Tester.** Did you know that you could get paid to try out a new website and give feedback? Sites like **UserTesting.com** are always looking for users to rate and give feedback about websites. Website owners post gigs to the site, and you simply login and give feedback and usability ratings on different websites and online apps. You can earn up to $10 for each test you participate in.

955. **Open a Profitable Game Store**. Video games sales today are bigger than all of Hollywood these days. Open up a shop that sells new and used PS4 or Xbox-1, Xbox-360 and Nintendo games and "cheat books" that teach the users how to win the games more easily or extend their lives in the games. You'll have a lot of gamers that should visit you in a mid-size city.

956. **Set up a business which produces coffee shop programs**. These programs might consist of 6-8 printed pages. Sell advertising space in these programs to local businesses along the sides of the programs. Make this entertaining facts and jokes, so that restaurant goers have something to read while waiting for their food. Restaurant owners love these programs too. Customers can take these programs home too from the table display unit, free of charge.

957. **Original Oil Paintings.** Begin a business which sells original paintings on revolving credit basis. Almost everyone would like to own original oil paintings but are put off because of the high initial cost.

958. **Operate a Jewelry lucky grab basket**. Bring together a selection of enameled, sea-shell, bead and carved Jewelry in a box. Wrap the box and place in a large tub of sawdust. Passers-by at local craft fairs or flea markets are invited to pick a box for a small charge.

959. **Grant Writing for Non-Profit Organizations**. Non-profits, universities, hospitals and other community organizations all have a great need for grant money to supplement their budgets, but grants are notoriously tricky to write for the first time. If you have experience writing grants, or are willing to learn how to do it by practicing your skills without pay for a few non-profits, you can start a lucrative freelance grant writing business. According to **eHow.com**, grant writers can make anywhere from $40,300 to $67,000 a year.

960. **Elementary school teachers**. Teach young children the basic coursework in schools. For most schools you'll need a bachelor's degree and in many states a teaching credential. Also a substitute teacher, in most cases only needs a bachelor's degree. The pay for substitute teachers is in the $100-$150 a day range. For fulltime elementary school teachers, **Median annual earnings in 2014: $54,120.**

961. **High School Sports Coach**. Become a high school football or basketball coaching and earn extra money every season. Depending on the state you live in, the average football coach alone makes between $3700 (in 2014) to 120,000/year if you coach in Texas or Alabama where they take their football very seriously. Do coaching because you enjoy it and you like helping your players get better. Consider this if you have flexible schedule from 2-6pm weekdays during the season, and some weekends for tournaments. Lots of fun too.

962. **Content Creator.** This is all about creativity and writing. As marketing becomes more education-based and less sales-based, demand for business writers who specialize in blogs, newsletters, website articles, whitepapers, and special reports will also increase. There is no typical education for professionals who specialize in content creation. Most have at least a bachelor's degree, with additional education in areas of specialization but even that is not a necessity for those with specialized knowledge. Individuals in this field must have good communication and writing skills, and be highly creative and original. They must also be self-motivated and self-disciplined in order to meet their employer's deadlines.

963. **Set up a school of motor racing**. Offer potential students a weekend or week-long course about the practical and theoretical aspects of motor racing.

Cars can be rented and an upsell for the training given. Insurance and liability here is key.

964. **Start a school of hydroponic gardening**. The aims of your school might include: publishing booklets, producing audio CD's or MP3's, organizing holiday courses, giving personal tuition and selling supplies.

965. **Bottle sand from the beaches** of Ft. Lauderdale, Florida, Monterey, California, and other Spring break vacation areas where college kids want to remember a piece of their spring break history.

966. **Begin a mail or online business which promotes the craft of making Jack-in-the-boxes and other wooden toys**. In your catalog include a wide selection of: springs, boxes, design plans, materials for making the character in the box, etc. Advertise in crafts magazines.

967. **Design and manufacture wooden lap desks for putting on your lap while driving in cars**. These should be lightweight and easy to store in a car. They might be used by sales people to make notes about calls, business people to prepare for meetings and passengers to work from whilst travelling.

**968. Bring out a selection of hanging cotton yard flags**. These are like flags or banners which are printed with a greetings message and can be hung from a ceiling or a rail. Arrange for these to be stocked at shops which sell greeting cards.

**969. Pet Sitting Service**. Perhaps you love dogs and cats. Perhaps you have some of your own and the idea of taking care of a few more for a few days appeals to you. Pet care needs continue to soar in the United States. Most people prefer the option of their pets being cared for in a loving home environment while they are at work or on vacation. These things mean that a home based pet care business can get off and running immediately. Easy to begin, with no licensing in most states. Liability insurance is inexpensive so make sure you have some.

**970. Begin a business which sells exotic plants to image conscious local businesses**. Call office-to-office and offer to bring a selection of plants on a trial basis, for example 10 days, free approval without obligation. Either rent and maintain those in each business or sell them directly to the business and let them maintain them.

**971. Start a service which does auditions of voices and music.** A person or a musical group records their voice on a CD/MP3 or video text and sends it to you. You make an assessment of the performance, for a fee, and critique them and make suggestions. Advertise your service in music publications. If the music is good, offer to represent them as their agent or manager, Get them gigs in the area.

**972. Mow lawns and do specific gardening and landscape work.** Place advertisements in the windows of local nurseries which read 'Best Lawn Cutting- Cheap' and state an hourly rate. When you visit customers, offer to cut their lawn on a regular basis. Discount a longterm 12-month contract by 10-20%

**973. Plus Size Clothing Store.** Plus Size stores are not new but still one of the top business ideas this year. Each year there are more calls for inclusion and diversity. More retailers are expanding their store collections to include clothing that fits every "body." Since more manufacturers are offering greater size collections, there's also more variety in clothing styles. Plus size clothing, as a standalone niche, allows you to fine tune your marketing directly to the plus sized audience. It allows women to shop on a website, for example, without worrying about finding the right size. You could expand to this business idea and also add plus sized clothing to your fashion store. However, avoid creating categories called 'Plus Sized Clothing.' Plus sized clothing can be marketed in countless ways. As a fashion business idea, you can also successfully market on Facebook or Instagram, especially, help skyrocket your pages engagement over time. Also market it as Plus-Size Shops for discriminating women who demand style.

**974. Set up a service which supplies sliced and seeded lemons to bars, restaurants, night-clubs and hotels.** In the course of an evening some bars use a large quantity of sliced lemons. These establishments could benefit from the convenience of having the lemons ready-sliced.

**975. Start a dial-a-gardener service.** Do you have a green-thumb? Do you love gardening and the outdoors? A single telephone call to you will send a gardener to a customer's home. Employ teenagers, students and retired people to do all the gardening with your oversight. Broker the gardening business and take 20-30% of the wage you receive from the client.

**976. Dog Breeding.** Earn a nice regular income from your special breed of dogs. Certain dog breeds can fetch $1000-$2000 a puppy. Advertise online at your website or at Craigslist.

**977. Bring together a selection of the best business audio CD's or MP3's from the previous year.** These can be from best leaders in the business world to local leaders that people want to learn from. Start a direct mail campaign which offers these CD's or MP3's to businesspeople at a reduced rate if they buy the set.

978. **Start a flowers of the week, month or quarter club**. Clients can place a standing order with you for the delivery of flowers at regular intervals.

979. **Vape Shop**. E-cigarettes are big business now with sales from convenience stores, tobacco shops and vape shops. Though this might seem like a real niche market for a small town business, the reality is that the vaping industry (and community) is currently exploding in the U.S. To give you a sense of how big the vaping market is, Quartz reported that Yelp has **10,591 "vape shops,"** as of this writing listed in their database. Depending on where you are in the country, however, due to state regulations, opening a vape shop will be easier in some states than in others. **Vape Shops** are generally focused shops that are dedicated to newbies, offering starter kits, hardware, e-liquids of many types and flavors, usually a tasting bar, information, support and hand holding. On the other end they cater to the experts too. With more and more states opening up marijuana use for recreational use expect to see vape shops, at least for now, opening up more across the country and around the world. Tens of millions of users now worldwide.

980. **Opening up a taco, food truck or hot dog cart** might not have been first on your list of ideas for a successful small town business, but depending on the location of your

town, the seasonality of its residents, and the weather, starting a food truck business can be a great investment. Many small towns have vibrant communities, and often these include outdoor activities such as sporting events, festivals, fairs and markets. Having the ability the drive your business to where the crowds are means major cash in your pocket. Food trucks (and hotdog carts) also have the added benefit that they can be rented for special events. So for a small town that might lack a proper catering service, being able to hire a food truck for your son's bar mitzvah or daughter's quinceanera is a perfect local option.

981. **Set up and organize a home-visiting massage service**. Your business would find work for experienced masseuses. Get customers by placing ads in local newspapers and on Craigslist (who now charge for these ads). Take a slice of every massage you arrange for your massage therapists. Keep this legitimate and you'll succeed in almost any market.

982. **Open a press cutting research service** for stock market investors. Read the daily papers and make a note every time a public company is mentioned. When an investor requests information about a company, you photocopy all the cuttings which mention the name of that company.

983. **Fill beautifully decorated bags filled with aromatic herbs and potpourri** which are designed for hanging around the house or in cars. Add an elastic string to

each bag so that one pull will release some of the aroma into the air. Sell at craft fairs and Etsy and Craigslist.

984. **Set up a business which makes eye pads for sleeping, nightshirts and nightcaps**. Have these stocked at up-market clothes retailers.

985. **Be a diet consultant.** Earn money from guiding people through published diets. Also you might buy the recommended food at trade prices and sell it to your clients. Advertise your service locally and visit the homes of clients to give private consultations. Diet programs are very popular.

986. **Become a make-up consultant.** Advise women on what make-up suits their individual mix of: skin shade, hair and eye colors, nose and facial shape, etc. Once you have established your consultancy, make more money by teaching others to be make up consultants.

987. **Bring out a newsletter which gives amateur magicians** ideas for new tricks. Also sell advertising space to firms which have products to sell to amateur magicians.

988. **Vitamin Online Store**. Start an online business which sells vitamin pills. Produce a catalog which contains a far wider range of vitamin pills than is available at shops. Collect a percentage or affiliate fee for your sales or private label them yourself and promote heavily.

989. **Open a Thrift Store or Second-Hand Shop.** Every town needs at least one thrift store. Yes, there might be fewer people in a small town, or fewer stores and shops, but that doesn't mean that babies don't grow out of their onesies, that people don't buy new furniture and kids don't move off to college. In our capitalist society, fewer people doesn't always mean less stuff. So opening a second-hand store or thrift shop is a great way to help the people of your town recycle their unwanted items while giving those that might not have as much a less expensive shopping option. One reason why opening a thrift store in a small town is a great idea, is that much of the merchandise you sell you will receive via donations. This does present logistics to think about regarding how to regulate and keep track of inventory, but it also means that even though you sell items for less than a traditional store, you'll never owe money to a middleman or manufacturer. You gotta love it. Some of my favorite places in the world to shop in the world are thrift stores.

990. **Be a home wig and hair consultant**. By visiting the homes of potential buyers you provide a private and confidential service which is free of embarrassment. Buy a selection from wigs from manufacturers at trade prices. Advertise your service in newspapers and magazines.

991. **Write and publish a monthly newsletter which helps those who want to give up smoking**. The ability to give up smoking depends on what's happening in a person's mind. Smoking today cost smokers, over $7,000 smoking just one pack per day for a year. This newsletter could make the difference between success and failure, life and death. Add years to your life and life to your years. Quit smoking now. See this author's page for his latest Stop Smoking Book here, **https://amzn.to/2HB89ZN**.

992. **Begin a confidential newsletter about how to get the best things from life**. The best things in this case include: money, expensive property, and respect and quality cars. Your newsletter should suggest some of the legal short cuts which can be taken. Provide case studies. Show the secrets of the most successful in your community or around the world.

993. **Open a Car Wash.** Whether a small town is in Kansas, Arizona or South Florida, one thing is for sure: people prefer shiny cars to muddy, rusty wrecks. It's just how we think about our cars right? You make your car payment every month, so your vehicle might as well shine! If there isn't a car wash in your town already or at least one in the next town over, opening a cash wash might be your perfect business opportunity. One thing to think about before getting started is:

location, location, location. Nail this stage of the planning and you'll make the rest of your ride significantly easier. Self-service car washes are popular everywhere or spend more and do a full service car wash. This business, with the right location, can really clean up.

994. **Movie Experience Shop.** In a city where there are many theatres, open a small shop (or online presence) which is devoted to selling things related to the movie experience. Tickets to all the productions, T-shirts, memorabilia etc., can be a fun place to begin or end your movie going experience.

995. **Publish a newsletter and blog/vlog for expectant mothers**. Provide subscribers with information and reassurance. Send each subscriber an issue which ties in with the stage of her pregnancy.

996. **Term Paper and Manuscript Service**. Use your computer and printer and provide a letter, term paper and manuscript typing service. Customers would be students, academics, writers who'd prefer others type out their book ide and small business people who have a need for clerical and typing work to be done by contract.

997. **Arrange for ink drawings to be made of historical characters** from all parts of the nation. There might be hundreds of drawings. Have these printed and framed and sell by mail order. The idea is that wherever a person is, they can

buy a framed drawing of someone famous from their own area.

**998. Start a life history photography service**. Produce an album of photographs which is a photographic history of a client's life. For example take photographs of a client's hospital of birth, former schools, places of work, place of marriage, houses they once lived in, etc.

**999. Take an attractive photograph of a large office block**. Frame enlarged copies and sell these to people who work there. This would be a good sideline business. If you work in an office block and you meet many other office workers in the course of the day.

**1000. Bring out a regular publication for ambitious amateur musicians**. This publication might include ads from: 1) Employers seeking musicians. 2) Retailers selling equipment accessories and supplies. 3) People selling used equipment. 4) Musicians seeking to make contact with other musicians. Also publish interesting editorials and letters.

**1001. Internet Security Consulting**. If you're tech savvy and understand the ins and outs of internet and computer security, consider becoming a consultant for small businesses. Unlike the big boys, these companies can't afford the huge security budgets, but they still want to be able to protect their internet customers and can make personal house calls to their clients, something in high demand these days. A monthly contract can be auto-billed monthly for your clients.

**Congratulations! You finished the book!** If you've read it straight through that's awesome. Hopefully you have found an "actionable business idea" (or several) that can get you moving towards your goal of becoming a business owner and then to create that perfect lifestyle.

*Now go over the book one more time and this time, really sort for the "best of the best."* Find that one business that you can begin to research, think about fully, and then commit to doing something to further that business's development. Take a day or two and digest what you've read. Don't procrastinate here. Let your subconscious mind direct you here.

Set a time and date to start your detail work on your business. You'll want to check the viability of the business, the market, competition, market leader research, start-up costs, business operating expenses, profit potential and return on investment. Location may be an important issue to consider also. Is this business online or a brick-and-mortar business?

As these variables and facts become known to you, you'll determine if it's right for you or not. But do something to further its development. Do this until it feels right. When it feels like it should, launch it and move it forward. You will win in your own business as you commit to doing what it takes to win and "create value" for your clients.

Business ownership can be the vehicle to not only provide you with a significant income, freedom to be your own boss, tax benefits and the ability to make a real difference in your community, but can also provide you with the "perfect lifestyle" which is a great goal in and of itself. Let your business provide that for you. Good luck in your business. It's going to be great!

# Resources

To get you started here are some resources that will bring you up to speed on starting and managing your business. Begin your business journey with researching viability and outlook.

- **The Small Business Administration.** https://www.sba.gov/managing-business/running-business/marketing

- **NFIB- National Federation of Independent Business-** http://www.nfib.com/business-resources/

- **SCORE- Free Small Business Advice from Business Professionals.** https://www.score.org/

- **Occupational Outlook Handbook, from the Bureau of Labor.** https://www.bls.gov/ooh/

- **US Chamber of Commerce-** https://www.uschamber.com/

- **INC.** Small Business Ideas and Resources for entrepreneurs. http://www.inc.com/

- **Small Business Resources-**

- http://www.smallbusinessresources.com/

- **Small Business Trends-**
  . http://smallbiztrends.com/

- **Small Business America-**
  http://www.huffingtonpost.com/news/small-business-america/

- **Entrepreneur Magazine-**
  https://www.entrepreneur.com/

- **The Self-Employed-**
  https://www.theselfemployed.com/

- **US Department of Labor-**
  https://www.dol.gov/oasam/programs/osdbu/sbrefa/

- **Business USA-** http://business.usa.gov/

- **LinkedIn Small Business-**
  https://smallbusiness.linkedin.com/

- **Gale Small Business Resource Center-**
  http://solutions.cengage.com/BusinessSolutions/Resource-Center/

- **HUD- Department of Housing and Urban Develpment-**
  http://portal.hud.gov/hudportal/HUD?src=/program offices/sdb/resource/guide

- **Legal Shield-** https://www.legalshield.com/

- **Legal Zoom-**
  http://businessresources.legalzoom.com/

- **Costco Wholesale Club-** http://www.costco.com/

- **Sam's Club-** http://www.samsclub.com/sams/

- **Forbes 30 Terrific Tools For Small Business-**
  http://www.forbes.com/sites/jasonnazar/2013/05/28/30-terrific-tools-for-small-businesses/#ec37866281a4

- **Post Planner- 20 Online Tools-**
  https://www.postplanner.com/top-20-small-business-tools-for-online-entrepreneurs/

- **Fundera- 50 Tools-**
  https://www.fundera.com/blog/2015/06/10/50-free-tools-to-help-grow-your-small-business/

- **Shopify-** https://www.shopify.com/blog/34283525-6-free-online-tools-every-business-owner-should-know-about

- **Business Plans-** http://articles.bplans.com/best-free-apps-online-tools-entrepreneurs-obsessive-collectors/

- **Reputation Loop-**
  https://www.reputationloop.com/best-small-business-tools-for-2016/

- **FreshBooks- 35 Tools-** https://www.freshbooks.com/blog/35-must-have-tools-for-small-business-owners/

- **Practical ECommerce-** http://www.practicalecommerce.com/articles/80188-20-Tools-to-Run-a-Small-Business

- **Small Business CEO-** http://www.smbceo.com/free-small-business-tools/

- **Next Day Flyers- Printing-** http://www.nextdayflyers.com/,

- **Vista Print-** Business Cards, Postcards, etc.- www.vistaprint.com

- **Cheapest Signs & Banners & Websites-** http://patriotwebdesign.com/

- **UPS- Shipping-** https://www.ups.com/

- **USPS- United States Postal Service-** https://www.usps.com/

- **Federal Express-** http://www.fedex.com/

- **Amazon-** https://www.amazon.com/

- **Ebay-** http://www.ebay.com/

- **Alibaba-**
  https://www.alibaba.com/countrysearch/CN/shopping-online-websites.html

- **Office Depot/ Office Max-**
  http://www.officedepot.com/

- **FREE Websites.** Yola, Weebly, Wix, Site123, and Website.

Please leave *positive feedback* and your comments if you've purchased **1001 Business Ideas** on Amazon and have found value in some of the ideas. Thank you so much. Also, please check out some of my other selections too. I hope you'll find them timely, well researched, helpful and easy to read. Be a good student too and learn all that you can about the business and industry you'll be starting.

**Bob Armstrong**

# Bonus

## Top 33 Best Free Classified Ads Posting And Listing Web Sites

**Which are the best free classified ads posting sites on the web?** Undeniably this is one of the most frequently asked questions among advertisers, bloggers and online marketers who want to post free classifieds ads for their blogs, websites, products, services, jobs, and houses.. Here we've compiled a list of **33 most popular free classified ads** sites where people can browse, view, and post ads, buy or sell any items they want.

All the sites listed below are high in both Alexa ranking and Google PageRank. If you post ads on one of these classified sites, you'll get a high chance of somebody viewing your ad and make a positive response. In short these sites are all well maintained and have high daily traffic which is absolutely worth your time and effort.

## 1. Craigslist

Craigslist is the largest and one of the most popular free classified advertisements sites with sections devoted to jobs, housing, and personals, for sale, services, community, and discussion forums.

## 2. KiJiJi – Free Classified in Canada

The most famous classified site in Canada to find a wide range of deals on local items from clothes to cars to apartments is Kijiji. The classified advertising service connects with local buyers and sellers, and shop through hundreds of categories. KiJiJi classified services are now available for more than 300 cities in Canada, Italy, Hong Kong, Taiwan and United States.

## 3. Gumtree

Gumtree is a famous free classifieds site in United Kingdom where users can buy and sell cars, flats and houses, services, pets and more.

## 4. FreeAdsTime

FreeAdsTime has included term free ads into their domain name to ensure that their services always will be provided at no charge. You're almost guaranteed to find all the major cities such as Los Angeles, Chicago, or Houston on this classifieds. It's local and easy to use, try it today.

## 5. Sulekha

Sulekha is a digital and mobile platform to connect people and businesses for local services. Users can post their ads in classifieds, find good roommates and low rentals, job offers, day care and anything you need in the daily life.

## 6. VivaStreet

VivaStreet enables users to browse the latest free classified ads in your area. The classified site covers a wide variety of adverts from used cars to properties to rent to pets for sale, etc.

## 7. AmericanListed

AmericanListed provides millions of safe and local classifieds for jobs, rentals, pets, for sale, housing, real estate, cars, boats, services, events, clothing, furniture and motorcycles.

## 8. ClickIndiaClassifieds

ClickIndia is one of the leading Classifieds sites in India. Users are allowed for online posting free classifieds for cars, houses, jobs, any products and services. The free ad posting site facilitates finding buyers, sellers, free advertisements and business promotions.

## 9. Click.in

Free Classified Ads India Similar to ClickIndia, Click.in is another reputable free classified ads site in India. The ad posting service lets you search and post free classifieds for flat, apartments, jobs, cars, travels and many more.

## 10. ClassifiedAds

The site name is very self-explanatory, another popular free classified ads platform for cars, jobs, real estate, pets, services, etc. Users can find what they are looking for or create their own ad for free.

## 11. Oodle

Oodle is one of the largest classifieds sites that aggregates listings from sites like eBay, ForRent.com, Myspace, as well as listings from local newspapers and websites. User can visit the site to find used cars, apartments for rent, job listings, homes for sale, and other classifieds.

## 12. Hoobly

Hoobly is a free classified ads site, with popular categories like arts, books, clothing, electronics, home and garden, pets, real estate, vehicles, etc.

## 13. Adpost

Adpost is a free classifieds site for over 1000+ cities, 500+ regions worldwide and across the world.

## 14. Salespider.com

Salespider.com is one of the largest free social network for business owners and includes free sales leads and prospect lists, free classified ads, free business directory, and free business forums.

## 15. OLX.com

OXL.com hosts free user-generated classified ads for communities around the world and provides discussion forums sorted by topics like cars, jobs, apartments, housing, pets, personals, and other categories. On OLX you can design ads with pictures and videos, control your selling and buying, display ads on your social networking profile and more.

## 16. Global-Free-Classified-Ads.com

Another popular free classified ads site where you can post free classified ads for cars, jobs, real estates, etc. for free.

## 17. Locanto Free Classified

Locanto is another worldwide online classifieds network for placing free classified ads for any items, services, for jobs, for dating, find good housing, lovely pets and more.

## 18. Claz

Claz.org lets you search all classified ads sites at once.

## 19. IndoClassified.com

IndoClassified.com provides free classified ads platform where anyone can post free ads in various categories such as For Sale, Vehicles, Classes, Real Estate, Services, Community, Personal and Jobs, browse through their huge selection of listing and find what you are looking for or sell your used goods at the best prices.

## 20. Yakaz

Yakaz is the search engine for all local classified ads on the web. Its categories include cars, motorbikes, housing, and more.

## 21. AdLandPro

With AdLandPro, you can post free classified ads, local classifieds and do free online promotion of your business with online business ads or classified posting.

## 22. Geebo

Geebo offers US's nationwide free classifieds for housing, rentals, roommates, employment, jobs, vehicles, autos, sales and more.

## 23. USFreeAds

USFreeAds is literally one of the biggest classified ads sites around and lots of products and services are being marketed there.

## 24. ClassifiedsForFree

Classifieds For Free is an online ad site for business opportunity, personal ads, auto, pets, real estate, and more. The site lets you post unlimited free ads and local ads in 600 US cities, all US States, and 60 countries.

## 25. PennySaverUSA

PennySaverUSA is another site where you can post and browse online classifieds, coupons, and more for free.

## 26. Khojle

Free Classified Ads in India. As the name implies, Khojle provides reliable facility to search classified ads in India. You can post free classified ads for job advertisements, sale of real property, cars, bikes, etc.

## 27. Clickooz Classifieds India

This is India free classifieds site that lets you post and browse classified ads under the categories of auto, real estate, pets, furniture, electronics and more.

## 28. Sell

Sell.com is a merchant advertising and e-commerce site where you can sell and buy electronics, pets, cars, computers, homes and more.

## 29. Adsglobe

Adsglobe is another advertising gateway for online classifieds in jobs, real estate, rentals, autos, and services, items for sale, travel, events, pets, business, and community.

## 30. IndiaList

This free classifieds portal in India lets you place free ads online for purchasing or selling any items and services. You may consider to post premium ads with extra features such as uploading more photos, and your ads will be shown at the top of search results.

## 31. FreeClassified

This site enables you buy or sell anything for free, place free local classified ads as well as search free local classifieds.

## 32. Loot.com

Loot.com is one of the best classifieds sites in the UK. The web portal is user-friendly, just post a free classified ads to purchase, sell, rent items, cars, properties, and find or offer jobs in your area.

## 33. WebClassifieds.us

A free classifieds site that lets you buy, sell and trade all types of items.

(Note: This article was updated on February 14, 2018) From: https://bit.ly/2HzVIuQ

# 50 Quotes to Inspire YOU
# The Entrepreneur

"Chase the vision, not the money; the money will end up following you." **–Tony Hsieh, Zappos CEO**

"Your work is going to fill a large part of your life, and the only way to be truly satisfied is to do what you believe is great work. And the only way to do great work is to love what you do." **– Steve Jobs, Co-Founder, Chairman and CEO, Apple**

"When you find an idea that you just can't stop thinking about, that's probably a good one to pursue." **–Josh James, Omniture CEO and Co-Founder**

"The critical ingredient is getting off your butt and doing something. It's as simple as that. A lot of people have ideas, but there are few who decide to do something about them now. Not tomorrow. Not next week. But today. The true entrepreneur is a doer, not a dreamer." **–Nolan Bushnell, Entrepreneur**

"It's almost always harder to raise capital than you thought it would be, and it always takes longer. So plan for that." — **Richard Harroch, Venture Capitalist and Author**

"Don't worry about failure; you only have to be right once." — **Drew Houston, Dropbox Co-Founder and CEO**

"Ideas are hard. Implementation is easy. There's always someone out there who can do what you need to have done." **–Bob Armstrong**

"Any time is a good time to start a company." **–Ron Conway, Noted Startup Investor, SV Angel**

"I knew that if I failed I wouldn't regret that, but I knew the one thing I might regret is not trying." **–Jeff Bezos, Amazon Founder and CEO**

"Act enthusiastic and you will be enthusiastic."**–Dale Carnegie, Author and Motivational Speaker**

"The way to get started is to quit talking and start doing." — **Walt Disney, Co-Founder, Disney**

"Remember to celebrate milestones as you prepare for the road ahead." **–Nelson Mandela, South African Leader**

"A pessimist sees the difficulty in every opportunity; an optimist sees the opportunity in every difficulty." **–Winston Churchill, British Prime Minister**

"User experience is everything. It always has been, but it's undervalued and underinvested in. If you don't know user-centered design, study it. Hire people who know it. Obsess over it. Live and breathe it. Get your whole company on board." **–Evan Williams, Co-Founder, Twitter**

"What do you need to start a business? Three simple things: know your product better than anyone, know your customer, and have a burning desire to succeed." **–Dave Thomas, Founder, Wendy's**

"As long as you're going to be thinking anyway, think big." — **Donald Trump, U.S. President**

"Whether you think you can, or think you can't -- you're right."
**–Henry Ford, Ford Motor Company Founder**

"You shouldn't focus on why you can't do something, which is what most people do. You should focus on why perhaps you can, and be one of the exceptions." **–Steve Case, AOL Co-Founder and CEO**

"Even if you don't have the perfect idea to begin with, you can likely adapt." **–Victoria Ransom, Wildfire Interactive Co-Founder**

"Don't limit yourself. Many people limit themselves to what they think they can do. You can go as far as your mind lets you. What you believe, remember, you can achieve." **–Mary Kay Ash, Mary Kay Cosmetics Founder**

"High expectations are the key to everything." **–Sam Walton, Walmart Founder**

"It's hard to beat a person who never gives up." **—Babe Ruth, Baseball Legend**

"Don't be afraid to assert yourself, have confidence in your abilities, and don't let the bastards get you down." **—Michael Bloomberg, Former Mayor of New York and Founder of Bloomberg L.P.**

"Trust your instincts."**—Estée Lauder, Founder, Estée Lauder**

"Make your team feel respected, empowered and genuinely excited about the company's mission." **—Tim Westergen, Pandora Founder**

"If you're not a risk taker, you should get the hell out of business." **—Ray Kroc, McDonald's Founder**

"The secret of getting ahead is getting started. The secret of getting started is breaking your complex overwhelming tasks into smaller manageable tasks, and then starting on the first one." **—Mark Twain, American Humorist and Author**

"Your most unhappy customers are your greatest source of learning." **–Bill Gates, Microsoft Founder and former CEO**

"Always treat your employees exactly as you want them to treat your best customers." **–Stephen R. Covey, Author**

"If you just work on stuff that you like and you're passionate about, you don't have to have a master plan with how things will play out." **–Mark Zuckerberg, Facebook Founder and CEO**

"In between goals is a thing called life that has to be lived and enjoyed." **–Sid Caesar, Entertainer**

"Wonder what your customer really wants? Ask. Don't tell." **– Lisa Stone, BlogHer Co-Founder and CEO**

"If you're passionate about something and you work hard, then I think you will be successful." **–Pierre Omidyar, eBay Founder and Chairman**

"Always deliver more than expected." **–Larry Page, Co-Founder, Google**

Waiting for perfect is never as smart as making progress." **–Seth Godin, Author**

"Every worthwhile accomplishment, big or little, has its stages of drudgery and triumph: a beginning, a struggle and a victory." **–Mahatma Gandhi, Political and Spiritual Leader**

One can get anything if he is willing to help enough others get what they want." **–Zig Ziglar, Motivational Speaker and Author**

"If everything seems under control, you're just not going fast enough." **–Mario Andretti, Legendary Race Car Driver**

"I'm convinced that about half of what separates the successful entrepreneurs from the non-successful ones is pure perseverance." **—Steve Jobs, Co-Founder and CEO, Apple**

"Never, never, never give up." **—Winston Churchill, British Prime Minister**

"The great personal fortunes in this country weren't built on a portfolio of fifty companies. They were built by someone who identified one wonderful business." **--THE TAO OF WARREN BUFFETT,**

"DON'T BE AFRAID TO TAKE TIME TO LEARN. I WORKED FOR OTHERS FOR 20 YEARS. THEY PAID ME TO LEARN." **--VERA WANG, DESIGNER**

"The value of an idea lies in the using of it." **—Thomas Edison, General Electric Co-founder**

"There's nothing wrong with staying small. You can do big things with a small team." **—Jason Fried, 37signals founder**

"Fail often so you can succeed sooner." —**Tom Kelley, Ideo partner**

"Stay self-funded as long as possible." —**Garrett Camp, founder of Expa, Uber and StumbleUpon**

"The only thing worse than starting something and failing... is not starting something." **—Seth Godin, Squidoo founder, author and blogger**

"Don't worry about funding if you don't need it. Today it's cheaper to start a business than ever." **—Noah Everett, Twitpic founder**

"We are really competing against ourselves, we have no control over how other people perform." **—Pete Cashmore, Mashable founder and CEO**

"Don't take too much advice. Most people who have a lot of advice to give — with a few exceptions — generalize whatever they did. Don't over-analyze everything. I myself have been guilty of over-thinking problems. Just build things and find out if they work." —**Ben Silbermann, Pinterest founder**

"There's lots of bad reasons to start a company. But there's only one good, legitimate reason, and I think you know what it is: it's to change the world." —**Phil Libin, Evernote CEO**

# Thank you!

## One Last Request Please...

If you have found value here, please leave a 5-Star review with our friends at Amazon. It really helps me to have great reviews from our best customers. Many thanks. ~Bob